CREATIVE
BIBLE LESSONS
ON THE
Prophets

12 sessions packed with ancient truth for the present

CRYSTAL KIRGISS

Youth Specialties

ZONDERVAN™

WWW.ZONDERVAN.COM

Creative Bible Lessons on the Prophets : 12 Sessions Packed with Ancient Truths for the Present

Copyright © 2002 by Youth Specialties

Youth Specialties Books, 300 S. Pierce St., El Cajon, CA 92020, are published by Zondervan, 5300 Patterson Ave. S.E., Grand Rapids, MI 49530.

Library of Congress Cataloging-in-Publication Data

Kirgiss, Crystal.
  Creative Bible lessons on the Prophets : 12 sessions packed with ancient truths for the present / Crystal Kirgiss.
    p. cm.
  ISBN 0-310-24137-5
  1. Bible. O.T. Prophets—Study and teaching (Secondary) 2. Christian education of teenagers. I. Title.
  BS1506 .K49 2002
  224'.0071'2—dc21

                                                                            2002004942

Edited by Tim McLaughlin
Cover design by Jack Rogers
Interior design by Razdezignz

Printed in the United States of America

  03 04 05 06 07 / VG / 10 9 8 7 6 5 4 3

To my three sons, Tyler, Tory, and Tate, who have the persistence of Jeremiah, the imagination of Ezekiel, and the honesty of Habakkuk— you keep me young.

To my husband, Mark, who has the integrity, wisdom and courage of Daniel—you keep me alive.

And to all those who faithfully pass on the stories and truth of the Old Testament prophets to each succeeding generation—you are the prophets of today, God's mouthpiece to the world.

—C. K.

CONTENTS

One Question: Why?!?

I know what you're thinking: *Why a book about prophets?* I mean, if given a choice between reading the Old Testament or the New Testament, most teens would choose the latter. If given the choice between reading the first half of the Old Testament (Adam, Noah, Joseph, Moses, and other biblical celebs) and the second half (prophet, prophet, prophet, and more prophets), most teens would choose the former.

So why in the world should anyone bother with this book—a study guide for teens on those crazy Old Testament prophets?

1. Because Jesus read and studied the prophets.

"He said to them, 'How foolish you are, and how slow of heart to believe all that the prophets have spoken! Did not the Christ have to suffer these things and then enter his glory?' And beginning with Moses and all the Prophets, he explained to them what was said in all the Scriptures concerning himself." Luke 24:25-27

2. Because the message of the New Testament is built on the foundation of the Old.

"Jesus replied: 'Love the Lord your God with all your heart and with all your soul and with all your mind.' This is the first and greatest commandment. And the second is like it: 'Love your neighbor as yourself.' All the Law and the Prophets hang on these two commandments." Matthew 22:37-40

3. Because the New Testament finishes a story that begins in the Old Testament.

"Do not think that I have come to abolish the Law or the Prophets; I have not come to abolish them but to fulfill them." Matthew 5:17

4. Because the prophets spoke the words of God.

"In the past God spoke to our forefathers through the prophets at many times and in various ways." Hebrews 1:1

"For prophecy never had its origin in the will of man, but men spoke from God as the Holy Spirit carried them along." 2 Peter 1:21

"In speaking, the prophet reveals God. This is the marvel of a prophet's work: in his words, the invisible God becomes audible." (The Prophets, 22)

5. Because the prophets reveal God's character to us.

Through the prophets, we see, hear, and experience God's loathing of injustice, his desire for fellowship with humankind, his intense, burning love for his creation, his desire for obedience, his jealousy and insistence on being recognized as the one true God, his sorrow for human suffering, his compassion, his mercy, his forgiveness, his fury, his faithfulness...in short, it's impossible to read the prophets and retain a narrow view of God's character.

"The pages of the prophetic writings are filled with echoes of divine love and disappointment, mercy and indignation. The God of Israel is never impersonal. The divine pathos is the key to inspired prophecy. God is involved in the life of man." (The Prophets, 24)

6. Because the prophets are more relevant today than ever.

Abraham J. Heschel, the well-known Jewish scholar, writes, "The things that horrified the prophets are even now daily occurrences all over the world...To us a single act of injustice—cheating in business, exploitation of the poor—is slight; to the prophets, a disaster. To us injustice is injurious to the welfare of the people; to the prophets it is a deathblow to existence...Their breathless impatience with injustice may strike us as hysteria...To the prophets even a minor injustice assumes cosmic proportions." (*The Prophets* 3, 4)

The prophetic writings teach loving God first and foremost, not some lifeless idol such as Baal or Asherah or (for today) The Gap or your Visa gold card. The prophetic writings teach loving and caring for others: widows, orphans, the homeless, and (for today) those with AIDS. The prophetic writings teach repentance and forgiveness. The prophetic writings teach righteousness and relationship. The prophetic writings teach the grind of daily living while keeping an eye on the promises of eternity.

That, for starters, is why someone should bother with this book.

Why a Book about These Particular Prophets?

Israel had a number of prophets early on in her history—Moses, Samuel, Nathan, Elijah, Elisha. This book is focused on the *writing* prophets, men who prophesied later in Israel's history and whose words are recorded in Old Testament books bearing their names. Two lessons are devoted to each of the Major Prophets (so named not because they are more important but because their books are longer)—Isaiah, Jeremiah and Ezekiel. The six remaining lessons cover Amos (man's injustice), Hosea (man's unfaithfulness, God's faithfulness), Jonah (God's love for all nations), Habakkuk (God's willingness to listen to our questions and complaints), Daniel (integrity, honor, and character), and Haggai and Zechariah (two different approaches to getting God's work done). The lessons, in case you're wondering, are ordered chronologically—not in biblical order. We believe the chronological order will give a better sense of historical continuity to this CBL edition.

(Oh yes...Joel, Obadiah, Micah, Nahum, Zephaniah, and Malachi weren't excluded for any other reason than space constraints. Perhaps they'll show up at another time in another book.)

Why a Book with So Many P's?

No reason, really. It just happened that way. It started with "prophet" and moved to words like "personal," "point," and "prayer." Then came "play" and "ponder." At that point (pardon the "p"), it seemed prudent (oops) to proceed (uh oh) as though that had been the plan (drat) all along. (Pardon the prolixity.) The final product (oh my) includes the following:

- **Prophet**—name of the guy the lesson is about
- **Prelude and Profile** (a.k.a., Preamble)—some basic facts about the prophet (and we're positivly serious when we note specific months when certain prophets did their stuff...that's based on solid, biblical scholarship)
- **Pundits**—informative quotes from theologians, scholars, and other such folk about the prophet
- **Purpose of Prophetic Pronouncements**—self-explanatory
- **Preview**—a quick overview of the book
- **Precepts and Principles**—poetry and prose from the prophet's writing (a.k.a., Scripture)

The above elements are intended as background info for the leader. Don't skip them. It's important to be as familiar as possible with each prophet. All of the above elements can also be used as teaching aids—print some quotes, hang them on the walls, and incorporate Scripture memory; use the Profile as a "10 Second Intro" for students; print copies of the Preview to use as Cliff's Notes, et cetera.

- **Play**—self-explanatory (remember to have music playing during these events)
- **Pause**—a moment's rest before moving from here to there
- **Ponder Points**—three main ideas in each lesson that you can pick and choose from
- **Personal Prescription**—an individual activity that helps students apply the lesson

As with all curriculum, the aforementioned elements are intended as guides *only*. Feel free to change, adapt, or rearrange anything and everything. You know your group best. If an idea won't fly with your students, skip it. If an activity seems too advanced, simplify it. (**A Note about Video Clips:** Before you look for them, be sure to set your timer on 00:00 when the film company logo is displayed—then scan for the given start-stop times.)

Your Responsibility

You can't wing a lesson about a prophet you're unfamiliar with. (Well, you can wing a lesson about a prophet you're unfamiliar with, but you'll be cheating both your students and yourself!) Here's a recommended plan of preparation:

1. If you've never read the specific prophetic book, by all means *read it*. All of it. Several times.

2. If it's been a while since you've read the specific prophetic book, refresh your memory by *reading it again*.

3. Gather a variety of study Bibles and read the appropriate book introduction. Some will be more informative/factual (NIV Study Bible) and some more casual/interpretive (Living Insights Study Bible). They're all worth the time and effort.

4. Familiarize yourself with the historical context of the specific prophetic book you're studying. It will be immensely helpful. (Remember that after Solomon's reign ended, Israel split in two. The Northern kingdom was known as Israel, and Samaria was the capital. The Southern kingdom was known as Judah, and Jerusalem was the capital. There was no love lost between the two. The Southern kingdom outlasted the Northern, but both were eventually conquered by enemy nations.) Understanding the historical and political situation surrounding each book is a must.

5. Read what other folks have to say about the prophets. Here are the works we consulted:

The Living Insights Study Bible, Charles R. Swindoll (Ed.), Zondervan, 1996; *NIV Study Bible,* 10th Anniversary Edition, Kenneth Barker (Ed.), Zondervan, 1995; *The Student Bible,* Philip Yancey and Tim Stafford (Eds.), Zondervan, 1986; *The Message: The Prophets,* Eugene H. Peterson, Navpress, 2000; *The Bible Speaks to You,* Robert McAfee Brown, Westminster Press, 1955; *The Story of Prophecy,* Hannah Grad Goodman, Behrman House, Inc., 1965; *The Old Testament Speaks,* 2nd Edition, Samuel J. Schultz, Harper and Row, 1960, 1970; *Prophets and Poets,* Grace Emmerson (Ed.), Abingdon, 1994; *All Things Weird and Wonderful,* Stuart Briscoe, Victor, 1981; *Preaching from the Minor Prophets,* Elizabeth Achtemeier, Eerdmans, 1998; *The Prophets,* Abraham J. Heschel, Prince Press, 2000 (Harper-Collins, 1962); *Classic Sermons on the Old Testament Prophets,* Warren W. Wiersbe (Ed.), Kregel, 2000; *And the Prophets,* Clovis G. Chappell, Abingdon, 1946; *The Sacred Sixty-Six,* Rolf E. Aaseng, Augsburg, 1967; *Your Key to the Bible,* Theodore Huggenvik, Th. D., Augsburg, 1944; *Our Old Testament Heritage I,* Terence E. Fretheim and Darold H. Beekmann, Augsburg, 1970; *Following God: Learning Life Principles from the Prophets of the Old Testament,* Wayne Barber, Eddie Rasnake, Richard Shepherd, AMG Publishers, 1999; *The Storyteller's Companion to the Bible: The Prophets I,* Michael E. Williams (Ed.), Abingdon, 1996; *Run with the Horses: The Quest for Life at Its Best,* Eugene H. Peterson, InterVarsity, 1983; *The Bible Jesus Read,* Philip Yancey, Zondervan, 1999; *Biblical Literacy: The Most Important People, Events, and Ideas of the Hebrew Bible,* Rabbi Joseph Telushkin, William Morrow and Co., Inc., 1997; *The Literary Guide to the Bible,* Robert Alter and Frank Kermode (Ed.), Belknap Press of Harvard University Press, 1987; *Who's Who in the Bible,* Peter Calvocoressi, Viking Press, 1987; *The Old Testament World,* John Roguson and Philip Davies, Prentice Hall, 1989; *The Kingdom of God and Primitive Christianity,* Albert Schweitzer, Seabury Press, 1968; *Zondervan NIV Bible Commentary,* Kenneth L. Barker and John R. Kohlenberger III, Zondervan, 1994

One more thought—the prophets offer so much more than descriptions of end times! If your students are genuinely interested in end-times doctrine, certainly don't ignore that interest. But be careful not to reduce a study of the prophets to wild imaginings about when and how the world will end. Yes, the prophets spoke about the future, but they *always spoke about the present condition of humankind in relation to God.* That's what your students should envision primarily when they think of the prophets—people who have vitally important things to say to each and every person alive today. —*Crystal Kirgiss*

In the Beginning...

...God created the heavens and the earth—and the people. God and the people were very much in love. Their favorite pastime was hanging out together. The relationship was—dare I say—perfect.

But then the people, in what proved to be habitual behavior, messed everything up. How? By putting more stock in what Satan said about God (because doesn't it make sense, after all, that Satan would know about such things...) than in what God said about God. After all, God only *made* the people, *fed* the people, *sheltered* the people, *protected* the people, and *loved* the people. Satan, umm, well, you know, seemed so smart and likeable and decent and honest. Who could blame the people for being so utterly duped?

Besides, everyone knows that an outside opinion (a.k.a., gossip) is so much more interesting and juicy (especially in fruit form) than plain, ol' solid truth. Indeed.

So God showed them the garden door and put the people in the world, which turned out to be a pretty yucky place no matter what Satan had said. Still, God tried to win their affection and hang out with them. And we all know how much people like to hang out with God. Every time God made some headway in his wooing of the people, the competing suitor stepped up his own wooing—which was not, and is not still, wooing at all, but rather a sordid seduction— and the people responded with, "Anyway, who wants to date a fuddy-duddy puritan like God who just wants to spend all his time talking about commitment and obedience and true love when we can date someone like Baal who knows how to party and have a good time? Bring it on, Baal!"

Enter the prophets. Each time the people seemed on the verge of a total breakup and rejection of God ("total" as in there was none of this "let's still be friends" rhetoric), a prophet appeared on the scene to speak the very words of God to his beloved.

It started with Moses, the original matchmaker, who first introduced the Hebrews to God and his offer of a monogamous, committed relationship. In the early ups and downs of the union, people like Deborah, Samuel, and Elijah helped steer the relationship to safety. But each time it seemed like things were really taking off, the people had second thoughts. The concept of having only one God as a mate seemed so, well, prudish and old-fashioned. ("Free love" was around long before the 1960s!)

About half a millennium after Moses first brought them back together, the people and God were really on the outs. Half the people were playing the now-that-I've-got-my-god, I-can-act-however-I-want game. The other half was playing the look-at-those-two-timing-people, we'd-never-be-like-them game. Things were definitely dismal. Worst of all, God's original plan of having his chosen people introduce him to all other peoples was in serious jeopardy. Why, after all that time, they barely even knew him! That'd be an awkward introduction.

So one by one, in a steady and unbroken thread, God continued sending his prophets to his chosen people in an attempt to save and strengthen the divine-mortal relationship. It was a lonely and discouraging job. One-sided attempts at reconciliation seldom succeed. But God is nothing if not faithful and persistent. Over and over again he proved his willingness to do whatever it took to convince the people of his love.

And as you know, Jesus (the greatest prophet of all) eventually arrived to finish and fulfill the job the prophets before him had begun—to reconcile people to God, once and forever, from now through eternity. Amen.—*C.K.*

JONAH The Unprophet

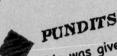

PUNDITS

He was given a ministry he did not want to a people he did not like.
Following God, 55

A Christian saying no to God is far more repulsive to the world than a pagan who lives an ungodly life.
Following God, 57

God's answer to Jonah, stressing the supremacy of compassion, upsets the possibility of looking for a rational coherence of God's ways in the world. History would be more intelligible if God's Word were the last word, final and unambiguous like a dogma or an unconditional decree. It would be easier if God's anger became effective automatically: once wickedness had reached its full measure, punishment would destroy it. Yet, beyond justice and anger lies the mystery of compassion.
The Prophets, 67

It becomes difficult to accept as members of the club people who have done nothing to qualify for membership.
Prophets and Poets, 242

Instead of being held up as an ideal to admire, we find Jonah as a companion in our ineptness. Here is someone on our level. Even when Jonah does it right (like preaching, finally, in Nineveh) he does it wrong (by getting angry at God). But the whole time, God is working within and around Jonah's very ineptness and accomplishing his purposes in him.
The Message, 500

PROFILE

- Jonah means "dove"
- Maybe wrote his own book...then again, maybe not
- Ministered between 800 and 750 B.C.
- Contemporary of Amos
- Only prophet whose main job was being God's mouthpiece to a foreign nation rather than to Israel/Judah
- In terms of repentance results, most successful prophet

PURPOSE OF PROPHETIC PRONOUNCEMENTS

TO DEMONSTRATE GOD'S LOVE FOR AND DESIRE TO FORGIVE ALL NATIONS.

- It's impossible to run away from God.
- Disobedience puts others in danger.
- Going your own way instead of God's way always takes longer and uses more energy.
- God's grace and mercy are available to everyone...even nasty Ninevites.

FROM OLD TO NEW
(where verses from this book are quoted in the New Testament)
Jonah 1:17 ↔ Matthew 12:40

PREVIEW
A PEEK AT THE PITH OF JONAH

Since everyone knows the story, here's the barest of possible previews—
• God tells Jonah to go up to Nineveh and preach repentance.
• Jonah says no.
• Jonah goes down to Joppa, down to the ship that's heading down to Tarshish, down to the hold, down for a nap, down to the sea, and down to the fish.
• God tells Jonah to go to Nineveh and preach repentance.
• Jonah says, fine, whatever, just lemme outta this fish!
• Nineveh repents.
• Jonah pouts.

PRECEPTS & PRINCIPLES
PRICELESS POETRY AND PROSE FROM JONAH

He said: "In my distress I called to the Lord, and he answered me. From the depths of the grave I called for help, and you listened to my cry." (Jonah 2:2)

When God saw what they did and how they turned from their evil ways, he had compassion and did not bring upon them the destruction he had threatened. (3:10)

Those who cling to worthless idols forfeit the grace that could be theirs. But I, with a song of thanksgiving, will sacrifice to you. What I have vowed I will make good. Salvation comes from the Lord. (2:8, 9)

PLAY
A TO Z VERSUS Z TO A

Ask for six volunteers (more or less, as time allows). Explain that the goal for each is to intelligibly recite the alphabet from A to Z in the shortest amount of time. One of the contestants should be a leader who's been prepped ahead of time to perform the required task *backward*. With a stopwatch, time all the contestants, one at a time, as they recite the alphabet. When it's the leader's turn, restate the goal, "Recite the alphabet from A to Z." You can preplan a short exchange that goes something like this:

You: *When I say GO, recite the alphabet from A to Z.*
Leader: *I don't want to.*
You: *But that's the way the game is played. You volunteered, remember?*
Leader: *Yeah, but now I don't want to.*
You: *Too bad. I need you to do this. So go already.*

Time the leader as she recites the alphabet—backward!

PAUSE

Segue from the alphabet stunt to the Bible-study part of the lesson by saying something like this:

It's always easier and faster to do things the right way. Reciting the alphabet from A to Z is fast and easy because it's the way we all learned it, and because it's the way it's supposed to be done.

We often think of prophets as men who did whatever God asked them, no matter how hard, strange, or difficult. Jonah was different. When God gave him a task, Jonah was determined to do the complete opposite of what God told him to do. In some ways, Jonah was an "unprophet," a man who disobeyed God, got angry with God, ran away from God—but still was used by God. Going our own way instead of God's way wastes time. Not to mention the trials, heartaches, and suffering to oneself and others it causes.

PONDER POINT - option 1
THIS SIDE DOWN

 "Whatever the original identification of Tarshish may have been, in literature and popular imagination it became a distant paradise." —C.H. Gordon (from *The Interpreter's Dictionary of the Bible*, as quoted in *Literary Guide to the Bible*, 235)

Have a student read Jonah 1:1-16. After the reading, ask students to identify the opposites they see in the story. They are—

- **Tarshish/Nineveh**
- **Land/Sea**
- **Sleep/Awake**
- **Unconcerned/Terrified**
- **Prayerless/Prayer to false gods**

Here are some interesting paradoxes to point out to your students—

- **Jonah, a landlubber, slept peacefully through the terrible storm. The sailors, seafaring pros, were terrified beyond words.**
- **Jonah, a prophet of the one true God, didn't pray during the storm. The sailors, followers of false gods, cried out in prayer.**
- **Jonah, a prophet who was called to lead others to God, was led to God by a pagan sailor (1:6).**
- **The sailors did everything in their power to save Jonah, a guy who put them as risk (1:13). Jonah did everything in his power to avoid saving the Ninevites, who never hurt him personally.**
- **The one place Jonah expected to be safe from what God was calling him to—a boat heading to Tarshish—was dangerous. The one place Jonah thought would be dangerous—the belly of a fish—was safe (and, in the end, saving).**

Divide students into groups of five or six. Give each group a copy of **This Side Down** (page 16). When groups have finished, discuss the following—

1. **Talk about a specific time when you tried to run away from or avoid God. Why did you do it? What happened as a result?**
2. **Of the instructions you talked about on the handout, are there any that you find especially challenging? Any that you really try to avoid? Why?**

3. What/where/who is your Tarshish (anything or anyone that you use as an escape from living out God's instructions)? In what ways does your Tarshish keep your mind off God?
4. When you avoid God's instructions or do exactly the opposite, what effect does it have on you? On God? On those around you?

PONDER POINT - *option 2*
WHO ARE YOUR NINEVITES?

Have a few students read the following verses—
- **Jonah 1:1-2**
- **Jonah 3:1-5**
- **Jonah 3:6-10**
- **Jonah 4:1-4**

Ask students to name different subcultures in their high schools—jocks, nerds, skaters, drama freaks, whatever. Then ask them to name other subcultures in society as a whole. List all of these on a marker board. Ask for a brief description of each group. Then discuss the following:

1. In your opinion, which of these groups are "bad"? Why? What makes a group "good" or "bad" according to the world? According to God? According to you? In other words, what are opinions based on when labeling or judging groups of people?
2. Which of these groups are the hardest for you to relate to? Why?
3. Which of these groups are the hardest for you to understand? Why?
4. Which of these groups are the hardest for you to communicate with? Why?
5. How do you either relate to or avoid specific groups?

Ninevites were *bad* people. Besides all of their pagan practices, they were also known for torturing and mutilating their enemies. They were easy to hate. And yet God loved them and wanted to save them.

Read the following sentence to your students having them fill in the blank silently.

I would rather that _____ [a group of people, or a specific individual] never learn about God and suffer the consequences than learn about his love and decide to follow him.

Now with the same group of people in mind, read the following to your students, and have them *write down* what they fill this blank in with.

I want _____ [a group of people, or a specific individual] to learn about God so much that I am willing to _____ [the steps of obedience you'll take].

PONDER POINT - *option 3*
WHAT IS YOUR VINE?

Give all students a copy of **This Fine Vine Is Mine** (page 17). Give them several minutes to work on it alone. When they're finished, regather in one group and have volunteers read the following Scriptures about heavenly versus earthly treasures—

- Colossians 3:1-3
- Matthew 6:19-21
- 1 John 2:15-17
- Philippians 3:18-19

Then discuss these things:

1. In today's world, what challenges do you face as you try to *not* focus on earthly things? Explain.
2. Do you think most of the people in your life (family, friends, peers, neighbors) have more than they need? Just enough? Not enough? Explain.
3. How does society define *essential*? In other words, what does the world say that you need? What does the world say that you deserve?
4. How do advertisers and the media try to convince people that they either need or deserve certain items? Do you think they're successful at this?
5. What are some ways you can fight obsessions with or desires of earthly things? What are some ways you can begin pursuing and obtaining heavenly things?

PAUSE

Segue into personalizing the lesson by saying something like this:

It's too bad that when people hear the name of Jonah, they usually think of a guy who got swallowed by a fish. This prophet's story has so much to say to us today, both about our relationship with God, our relationship with the world, and our relationship with others.

PERSONAL PRESCRIPTION
PUT YOURSELF IN THIS PARABLE

End this lesson by thinking a little more about the issue in Ponder Point/option 2. Jesus' parable of the workers (Matthew 20:1-16) is a perfect illustration. Not only does it teach that God desires and invites all kinds of people into his kingdom, but it also reprimands those religious people who grumble about God's expansive mercy. If Jonah were in the parable, he might have said, "God, it's not fair! I've worked for you my whole life—years and years. You can't hire the Ninevites this late in the game and pay them the same amount you're going to pay me!"

Read this parable in Matthew 20:1-16 to your students. Then give each a copy of **Put Yourself in This Parable** (page 18) and let them work on it alone or with a few other people.

Plus...encourage your students to read Psalm 139 this week as a reminder that it's impossible to run away from God. Is that a scary thought? If you're trying to avoid him, yes. When you consider that it means he'll never lose you in the crowd, no.

This Side Down

God gave Jonah specific instructions about his job as a prophet. He gives us specific instructions, too, about our job as his disciples and representatives in the world. It's easy to be like Jonah and avoid going in God's direction.

Look up the following verses and write down God's instructions to us about how to live and serve him. Then list ways that we try to avoid or do the opposite of what God tells us.

THE BIBLE REFERENCE	"WHAT GOD WANTS ME TO DO"	"HOW I AVOID DOING IT"	"WHAT I DO INSTEAD"
Matthew 5:43-48			
Ephesians 6:1-3			
James 1:22-26			
James 2:1-9			
1 Peter 3:8-17			

This Fine Vine Is Mine

Read Jonah 4:5-11. Think about the following things.

- Jonah built himself a shelter. He had all he really needed.

- God gave Jonah the vine for added comfort. It was extra, a gift.

- Jonah was happy about the vine. But was he thankful?

- When the vine died, Jonah wasn't sad. He was angry.

- Jonah's personal comfort was more important to him than the Ninevites' eternal condition

- Jonah was a selfish pouter who thought he deserved all the good things he could get his hands on.

Now answer this:

Here are some extra things in my life (not basics like food, clothing, and shelter) that I would be upset about losing or not having: [list some items here]

Now rank those things numerically: put a 1 next to those things you'd be most upset about losing, a 2 by those you'd be a little less upset about losing, etc.

Circle one:

I do / don't consider myself materialistic.

I do / don't consider things other than clothing, food, and shelter as nonessential extras.

I do / don't hold on tightly to the extra, nonessential things in my life.

I do / don't care about my personal comfort and happiness more than I care about others.

I would / would not be willing to give up my number-one extra if God asked me to.

Put Yourself in This Parable
(personal prescription)

Reread Jesus' parable. You can find it in Matthew 20:1-16. Think about people in your own life who fit these roles in the story (put yourself in one of the worker slots depending on how long you've been working for God/been a Christian)—

PARABLE PERSON	WHO IN YOUR LIFE FITS THIS ROLE?
Landowner	God
People who get hired first	
People who get hired second	
People who don't know about the landowner	
People who know about the landowner but don't realize that he's hiring	
People who think the landowner only hires trained farmers or gardeners	
People who aren't interested in working anywhere	
People who need a job but don't want to work for the landowner	
People who get hired in the middle of the day	
People who get hired near the end of the day	

Imagine you just heard Jesus tell this story.

What initial impression does it make on you?

What single idea or message does it give you?

What can you begin doing in response to that message?

How are you going to fight against the temptation to "run away" if and when you experience it?

AMOS
A Cry for Justice!

PUNDITS ✎

When the most vulnerable among us are treated unjustly—in the market-place, in our politics, in our hearts—we have committed the most egregious offense to Yahweh.
Storyteller's Companion, 167

[Amos contains] the most sustained statement of God's righteous judgment upon his own sinful people.
Prophets and Poets, 217

Justice is more than an idea or noun. Justice is a divine concern.
The Prophets, 32

Chosenness must not be mistaken as divine favoritism or immunity from chastisement, but, on the contrary, that it meant being more seriously exposed to divine judgment and chastisement.
The Prophets, 34

PROFILE

• A.k.a. "The Prophet of Doom"

• Prophesied between 750 and 760 B.C.

• A farmer and shepherd from Tekoa in the Southern Kingdom, or Judah (King Uzziah)

• Traveled to and prophesied to the Northern Kingdom, or Israel (King Jereboam II)

• Prophesied during a time of great prosperity and material wealth

• Prophesied to the very rich about their mistreatment of the very poor

• First prophet to have words recorded in book named after him

• Never claimed to be a prophet, only a shepherd to whom God said, "Go."

PURPOSE OF PROPHETIC PRONOUNCEMENTS

TO CHALLENGE MATERIALISM, IMMORALITY, AND INJUSTICE IN THE LAND OF ISRAEL.

• "Chosenness"—being God's people—does not give license to live unjustly.
• God's chosen people, like the rest of the world, will face God's judgment.
• If anything, God's chosen are called to higher standards of behavior than the rest of the world.
• God despises religious behavior that isn't genuine.
• God can use anyone, even a farmer, to speak his word of truth.

PREVIEW
A PEEK AT THE PITH OF AMOS

Amos, a shepherd and farmer from Judah (Southern Kingdom), was sent by God to prophesy to Israel (Northern Kingdom). Because of rivalries between those two kingdoms, he was probably considered a dubious character from the very start. On top of that, he was just an everyday sort of fellow claiming to speak a divine message. (The nerve!)

FROM OLD TO NEW
(where verses from this book are quoted in the New Testament)

Amos 5:25-27 ↔ Acts 7:42-43
Amos 9:11-12 ↔ Acts 15:16-17

So how did this good-for-nothin' Southerner grab the attention of his Northern audience? By cleverly and strategically pronouncing judgment on Israel's many enemies: "Doom to Damascus, Gaza, and Tyre! Doom to Edom, Ammon, and Moab!" "You go, Amos!" cheered the Israelites. To add to their frenzied excitement, he then pronounced judgment on Judah, that sniveling, do-gooding, high-and-mighty southern rebel. "Preach it, Amos! Amen!" cheered the Israelites.

Now that Amos had their attention and support, he did what he was sent to do—he pronounced judgment on Israel's lack of justice and compassion. "Yeah Amos! You da man! Down with Isra—hey! Wait a sec! He's talking about us! Doesn't he know we're God's chosen people!?!"

Amos then received three visions of Israel's demise. The first two—destructive locusts and consuming fire—prompted Amos to plead for God's mercy on the Israelites, even though they didn't deserve it. In both cases, God relented. But after the third vision, Amos didn't ask for mercy. Why? Because the image of a straight and true plumb line in the middle of crooked Israel convinced Amos that even the most merciful God could not be expected to overlook such wickedness.

When the local priest Amaziah heard what Amos was saying to his people, he did the typical holier-than-thou thing. He ignored the positive ("Seek the Lord and live") and whined about the negative ("Woe to you who are complacent in Zion").

"Stop this judgmental ranting at once and go back to where you came from," Amaziah told Amos. "You are a bad, bad person who obviously has some dysfunctional personal issues you need to work on."

Not long after that Israel fell to the Assyrian army, and the 10 tribes were exiled throughout the region—never again to be joined as a kingdom, just as Amos had prophesied.

Surprise, surprise.

PRECEPTS & PRINCIPLES ✏️
PRICELESS POETRY AND PROSE FROM AMOS

He who forms the mountains, creates the wind, and reveals his thoughts to man, he who turns dawn to darkness, and treads the high places of the earth—the Lord God Almighty is his name. (Amos 4:13)

Seek good, not evil, that you may live. Then the Lord God Almighty will be with you, just as you say he is. (5:14)

But let justice roll on like a river, righteousness like a never-failing stream! (5:24)

PLAY
VIDEO CLIP

Play the clip from the movie *Armageddon* in which Harry (Bruce Willis), a blue-collar kinda guy, arrives to tell know-it-all NASA geeks how things should be done. (23:10—27:39)

After you show the clip, talk with your students along these lines:

- *What does "from the wrong side of the tracks" mean? Describe the people usually given this label.*
- *Describe what it's like to be the outsider, the odd man out, the new kid in town.*
- *How do most people respond to the outsider, the odd man out, the new kid in town? Talk about that.*

PAUSE

Using the info from Profile, Pundits, Preview, and Precepts & Principles, introduce Amos as a prophet from the other side of the tracks (like Harry) who arrives in Israel (kind of like NASA) to tell the people (who, like trained astronauts and engineers, ought to know better) what's what.

PONDER POINT - option 1
BOTTOM TEN

Divide students into groups of about five. Give each group a copy of **Bottom Ten** (page 25). Let them spend about 10 minutes ranking their answers. Then regather, have each group share their responses, and discuss the following questions.

- *Talk about how you decided which item was the worst.*
- *What kind of injustices are most offensive to you personally? Explain.*
- *What kind of injustices do you think are most offensive to God? Explain.*
- *Do you think America is more / less / just as guilty of injustice as other countries? Talk about that.*
- *Are Christians and the church guilty of any social injustices? Explain why you do or don't think so.*
- *Some Americans enjoy great wealth and prosperity. Others are relatively well off. Many live comfortably with all their basic needs satisfied. Still others live at poverty level. Talk about how these different groups view one another and interact.*
- *Do you think the church should play a role in dealing with social injustices such as prejudice, hunger, homelessness, et cetera? Talk about that.*

PAUSE

End Ponder Point by saying something like this:

It's easy to point our fingers in condemnation at other countries and other people. We make careful note of all their mistakes and sins. Then we envision God's anger toward the evildoers. But in the process, we often ignore or deny our own acts of daily injustice and our own worship of material things.

PONDER POINT - *option 2*
NORTH VERSUS SOUTH

Amos told the Israelites about God's anger with the neighboring kingdoms, all of which were guilty of murder, rape, pillaging, slavery, and other atrocities. God promised to "send fire" on the cities, to "consume the fortresses," and to "destroy the kings." The Israelites were probably delighted with the message. Finally the other folks—the bad guys—were going to get what they deserved.

But Amos wasn't done. He had two more messages. The first was for Judah—Israel's southern counterpart, estranged relative, and uppity, do-gooding neighbor (see **North Versus South**). No doubt the Israelites jumped for joy when Amos pronounced judgment on Judah. Finally, the nasty neighbors were going to feel God's wrath. The irritating kingdom of Judah was finally pinned as the bad brother. Maybe now they, Israel, would be in line for providing the Messiah. The people of Israel had God right where they wanted him—on their side.

Or so they thought. Amos had one more message of doom and judgment...and guess who it was for?

Divide students into small groups and hand out **Right Road, Wrong Direction** (page 26). After students spend 10 minutes or so on it, regather as an entire group. Have each small group read their list aloud, then discuss the following:

1. What things on the list do you think are worst? Why?
2. Is anything on the list a problem in today's society? Talk about that.
3. Is anything on the list a problem for today's churches or Christians? Talk about that.
4. Talk about the way you think God views Christians versus the way you think God views non-Christians. How might this affect the way Christians and non-Christians interact?
5. Do you think wealth, material goods, and prosperity are good for the church, bad, neither, or both? Why?

NORTH VERSUS SOUTH

After Solomon's reign ended, Israel divided into two separate kingdoms (see 2 Chronicles 9:30-10:19). The Southern Kingdom, called Judah, included the tribes of Judah and Benjamin. The Northern Kingdom, called Israel, included the other 10 tribes of Jacob's sons. "So Israel has been in rebellion against the house of David to this day," wrote the chronicler (2 Chronicles 10:19). Furthermore, the prophets foretold that the promised Messiah would come from Judah. This didn't do much for Israel's self-esteem, nor did it breed warm, fuzzy feelings between the two kingdoms. Around 722 B.C. Israel was destroyed by Assyria, and the 10 tribes were scattered throughout the region, never again to be reunited as a kingdom. They are the famed "10 Lost Tribes of Israel" that have been spoken of ever since.

PONDER POINT - *option 3*
FAITH PYRAMID

Amos 8:5-6 paints a vivid picture of a "Sunday Christian." The New Moon and the Sabbath were official religious festivals. All business was suspended during those times so the people could concentrate on their worship. But while going through the motions of worshiping, a lot of them were mentally planning their workweek.

How often do today's churchgoers find their thoughts wandering to the afternoon ahead, to the Monday morning office meeting, to the tight schedule from Monday through Friday, and all sorts of other things?

Perhaps the hardest thing about being a Christian is being a Christian *all week long.*

Give each student a copy of **Faith Pyramid** (page 27). Give students a few minutes to fill it out, and then come back to discuss the following questions:

- *Identify when and where your faith is least active. Talk about the possible reasons.*
- *Identify when and where your faith is most active. Talk about the possible reasons.*
- *What is your definition of a "Sunday Christian"? Talk about that.*
- *Is "Sunday Christianity" more, less, or as much of a problem as it was in Amos' day? Talk about that.*

PAUSE

Segue into the next section, Personal Prescription, by saying something like this:

God is clearly disappointed and angry at the Israelites for their unjust and unkind behavior toward each another. He's also angry that they think so much of their material wealth and prosperity. Amos challenges all of us to examine how we treat one another. Does kindness define our attitudes? Or are we more me-centered? Do people know that you are Christians because they see your love for one another? Are non-Christians drawn to your Christlike attitude? Or do you live one life on Sunday and another during the rest of the week?

PERSONAL PRESCRIPTION
AMOS AND YOU

Give each student a copy of **Amos and You** (page 28). If it's appropriate, you might want to ask a few kids to share their responses. On the other hand, their responses may be very personal, in which case you will probably want to cut directly to the—

PRAYER

When students have finished their **Amos and You** handouts, close in a time of prayer. You can break up into small groups or stay in one large group. If a student or leader is willing, ask them to pray. Otherwise, close with a prayer like this—

Dear God,
Thank you for your Word. Thank you for speaking to us personally and showing us how to live. This week, give us the wisdom and courage to follow the message of Amos. Help us show kindness to the people we are with. Help us treat others fairly. And most especially, help us carry our faith with us always, not just when we are in church. Amen.

Bottom Ten

Rank the following acts by degree of evilness (1 = least evil, and 10 = the worst, most sinful, most offensive to humanity, most angering to God).

The Holocaust during World War II
1 ◆ 10

Slavery in America
1 ◆ 10

Ethnic cleansing
1 ◆ 10

Religious persecution
1 ◆ 10

Nuclear warfare
1 ◆ 10

Child labor
1 ◆ 10

Sweatshop working conditions
1 ◆ 10

Prosecution for a crime with no trial by jury
1 ◆ 10

Racial profiling
1 ◆ 10

Making profits off timber, jewels, et cetera, by ravaging the environment
1 ◆ 10

Terrorist attacks
1 ◆ 10

Be sure you can defend your choices

Right Road, Wrong Direction

Read Amos 2:4-3:12, God's words of judgment against his chosen people in Judah and Israel.

The Israelites had been specially selected and chosen by God. By calling them his people, he'd put them on the right road for good living. But being on the right road wasn't enough. God also expected his chosen people to travel in the right direction. And so far, they'd failed miserably. Look at the following verses that describe Judah's and Israel's sins. Make a list of those sins next to each Bible reference.

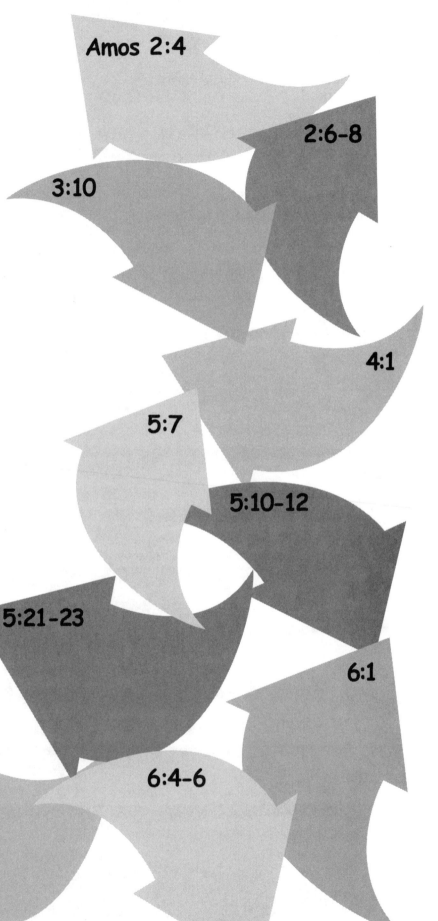

Amos 2:4

2:6-8

3:10

4:1

5:7

5:10-12

5:21-23

6:1

8:4-6

6:8

6:4-6

Faith Pyramid

When, where, and with whom does your faith take center stage? Fill in this pyramid with different aspects of your life so that the bottom of the pyramid represents where you are most faithful, and the top represents where you are least faithful. Think about how active your faith really is (as opposed to how active it should be) in each situation. Be honest!

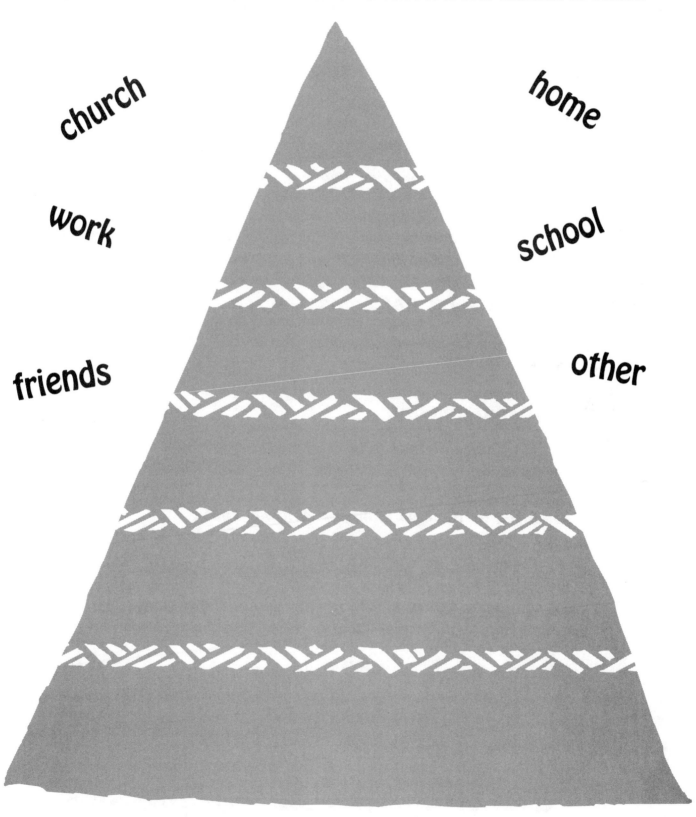

church

home

work

school

friends

other

Amos and You
(personal prescription)

Think about the message of Amos...

Live justly and righteously.

Treat others kindly and fairly.

Don't let material possessions divert your attention from relationships.

Make sure God is a day-by-day, minute-by-minute priority, not just a short pit stop on Sunday mornings.

Think about the person of Amos...

An ordinary guy who, when God gave him an extraordinary task, said, "Okay."

Now think about yourself...

What part of Amos' message is speaking to you?

What can you do to begin changing behavior that God might be displeased with?

Write a brief message to yourself below about those things. Be sure to think and pray about this issue during the week.

HOSEA
Only Love Can Break Your Heart

PUNDITS

...there is at least one Israelite [Hosea] who fully understands the pain and betrayal God feels because of the Israelite's repeated reversion to idolatry.

Biblical Literacy, 310

The covenant relationship in Hosea and, indeed, throughout much of the Old Testament is seen not as a legal contract fulfilled by obedience or the law, but a relationship of the deepest intimacy and love.

Preaching from the Minor Prophets, 6

Despite God's condemnation and the harshness of language with which the unavoidable judgment was announced, the major purpose of the book is to proclaim God's compassion and love that cannot—finally—let Israel go.

NIV Study Bible (10th Anniversary Edition), 1313

PROFILE

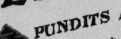

• Hosea means "salvation"

• Prophesied mainly to Northern Kingdom (Israel)

• Only writing prophet to actually come from the Northern Kingdom

• Uses the word return 22 times

• Prophesied around 760-720 B.C.

• Perhaps more than any other prophet, personally understood and experienced God's feelings

• Married a prostitute named Gomer

• Prophesied during the dark years immediately preceding Israel's defeat and exile

• Contemporary of Isaiah, Amos and Jonah

PURPOSE OF PROPHETIC PRONOUNCEMENTS

TO CONVEY THE DEPTH OF GOD'S LOVE FOR HIS CHOSEN, THOUGH UNFAITHFUL, PEOPLE.

• God desires return and reconciliation.
• God not only loves his people—he's in love with his people.
• God is faithful even when his people are not.
• Sin makes the heart callous and cold.
• Irreconcilable differences are, in fact, reconcilable.

PREVIEW
A PEEK AT THE PITH OF HOSEA

God chose Hosea to accuse and warn Israel about a great sin—unfaithfulness to the Lord. God wanted Hosea to understand how deep his love was for Israel and how intense his pain was because of her unfaithfulness. So God told Hosea to live out a similar experience: to marry a prostitute who would inevitably be an unfaithful spouse.

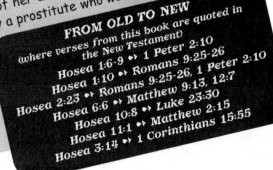

FROM OLD TO NEW
(where verses from this book are quoted in the New Testament)

Hosea 1:6-9 ↔ 1 Peter 2:10
Hosea 1:10 ↔ Romans 9:25-26
Hosea 2:23 ↔ Romans 9:25-26, 1 Peter 2:10
Hosea 6:6 ↔ Matthew 9:13, 12:7
Hosea 10:8 ↔ Luke 23:30
Hosea 11:1 ↔ Matthew 2:15
Hosea 3:14 ↔ 1 Corinthians 15:55

So Hosea chose Gomer, and they eventually had three children. (Actually, there is some scholarly debate about whether Hosea was actually the father of all three.) After a while, Gomer left Hosea and had affairs. God told Hosea to love Gomer as much as he, God, loved Israel and to take her back as his wife again. The story of Hosea's love affair with Gomer parallels the story of God's love affair with Israel—God loved and chose Israel, Israel rejected him, God continued to love her, she continued to reject him, and so on.

God pronounced judgment on Israel for her sin and declared that repentance is the only road to reconciliation.

PRECEPTS & PRINCIPLES
PRICELESS POETRY AND PROSE FROM HOSEA

I will betroth you to me forever; I will betroth you in righteousness and justice, in love and compassion. I will betroth you in faithfulness, and you will acknowledge the Lord. (Hosea 2:21)

For I desire mercy, not sacrifice, and acknowledgment of God rather than burnt offerings. (6:6)

For I am God, and not man—the Holy One among you. (11:9b)

But you must return to your God; maintain love and justice, and wait for your God always. (12:6)

But I am the Lord your God, who brought you out of Egypt. You shall acknowledge no God but me, no Savior except me. (13:4)

I will ransom them from the power of the grave; I will redeem them from death. Where, O death, are your plagues? Where, O grave, is your destruction? (13:14)

The ways of the Lord are right; the righteous walk in them, but the rebellious stumble in them. (14:9b)

PLAY - option 1
VIDEO CLIP

Play the clip from *My Best Friend's Wedding* in which Jules (Julia Roberts) is chasing a boy who's marrying a girl. (1:16:00—1:20:29) Introduce Hosea as a prophet who understood about loving someone enough to chase her down, even if it was humiliating.

PLAY - option 2
FAMOUS PAIRS

Have students get into groups of three or four. Hand out **Famous Pairs** (page 35) to each group and give them two minutes to work on it. Then give the correct answers (below) and compare scores.

Answers to Famous Pairs:
Jack and the beanstalk (fairy tale)
Bert and Ernie (*Sesame Street*)
Anthony and Cleopatra (history)
Scarlett O'Hara and Rhett Butler (*Gone with the Wind*)
Adam and Eve (Bible)
Clark Kent and Lois Lane (Superman)
Romeo and Juliet (Shakespeare)
Mike and Ike (candy)
Hansel and Gretel (children's story)
Calvin and Hobbes (cartoon)
Now and Then (movie)
Dr. Jekyll and Mr. Hyde (book and movie)
Ali Baba and the 40 Thieves (Arabian tale)
Lewis and Clark (explorers)
Peanut butter and jelly (food)
Stars and Stripes (U.S. flag)
Chutes and Ladders (board game)
Sweet and Sour (dipping sauce)
Vinegar and oil (salad dressing)
Chip and Dale (Disney cartoon)
Ben and Jerry's (ice cream)
Green Eggs and Ham (Dr. Seuss)

If you (or your students) want to, you can extend this game by challenging kids to call out the names of other pairs not on the list.
Then discuss the following questions—
• What things make for a successful pair? Explain.
• What things can make a pair unsuccessful? Explain.
• Does being part of a pair tend to enhance or diminish one's own identity? Talk about why you think so.

PAUSE

Segue from the Famous Pairs game to the Bible study part of the lesson by saying something like this:

Celebrities seem to become even more intriguing when they pair off. Movie stars, musicians, television actors, politicians, foreign royalty—whoever they are, we tend to be very curious and interested in the relationships of others, whether the details are real or fictitious. You want proof? Tabloids, TV Guides, celebrity Web sites, gossip columns, soap opera plots, best-selling romance novels, chick flicks—accurate or not, those relationships tend to be short-lived.

This lesson is about a guy in the Bible (and the God in the Bible) who went through a lot of heartache in his most important relationship.

Use the info in the Profile, Prelude, and Preview (earlier in this lesson) to give your students a quick peek at Hosea.

PONDER POINT - *option 1*

Have someone read Hosea 1:2-11 aloud to the entire group (see **Him? Marry Her?!**) Then discuss the following questions:

- *Why do you think God told Hosea to marry a prostitute? Explain.*
- *If Hosea was free to marry any prostitute, why do you think he chose Gomer? Explain.*
- *What do you think other people thought about Hosea and Gomer's relationship? Explain.*
- *In what ways can our lives, like Hosea's, reveal God's thoughts and feelings? Discuss.*
- *Some people think God unfairly "used" Hosea to make a point. What's your opinion?*

HIM? MARRY HER?!

There is some disagreement among scholars as to whether Gomer was a prostitute before her marriage to Hosea, or whether she was unfaithful only after her marriage. If Hosea's experience was meant to parallel that of God's, then one is inclined to think that Gomer was a prostitute before meeting Hosea. Her life of sin would have represented the fact that God chose Israel as his own in spite of her sins.

PONDER POINT - *option 2*

Without going into specifics, Hosea 3:1 makes it clear that Gomer had been unfaithful to Hosea. Discuss the following questions about Gomer's unfaithfulness:

- *List some possible reasons why Gomer might have left Hosea.*
- *What are some of the common reasons people give for leaving a serious or marriage relationship? Which ones seem legitimate? Which ones seem like excuses? Talk about this.*
- *Many people leave because they're "looking for something more." What do you think they're looking for? Do you think they find it? Discuss this.*
- *Why do you think so many relationships are short-lived?*
- *What things do you think are necessary for a life-long, committed relationship?*

CELEB BREAKUP

To help start this discussion, find a current story about a famous couple's breakup and read some or all of it to your students. (Virtually any issue of **"People"**, **"Us"**, **"Entertainment Weekly"**, et cetera, should carry such news.) Be sure the story includes things like the cause of breakup, excuses for the breakup, accusations, and the like.

Gomer's unfaithfulness to Hosea parallels Israel's unfaithfulness to God. Divide into small groups. Give each group a copy of the discussion starter **I Do, I Don't** (page 36).

PONDER POINT - *option 3*

Gomer was ultimately reunited with Hosea, but only because Hosea made the first move. He searched for Gomer, found her, and brought her back home again.

Have someone read Hosea 3:1-3 to the group. Then ask the following questions:

- *Compare Hosea's reconciliation with Gomer to Jesus' reconciliation with humankind. Talk about any similarities, parallels, et cetera.*
- *What is your reaction to this statement? "I am no better than a prostitute who has deserted her husband and slept with many other men...and yet Jesus loved me enough to buy me back as his own."*

Now have someone read Hosea 2:14-20 to the entire group. Then ask the following questions:

- *Describe God's plan for winning back Israel's love and devotion. [It might help if you have your students make a list of descriptive phrases from the passage, such as "allure her," "lead her," "betroth," et cetera.]*
- *Compare the relationship between a husband and wife with the relationship between God and Christians (or the church). Describe any similarities and differences.*
- *How does this image of God as husband/lover fit into your image of him? Talk about this.*

PAUSE

 Segue into the next section, Personal Prescription, by saying something like:

While Amos emphasized the things that God had done for Israel, Hosea emphasized the depth with which God loved Israel. While Amos emphasized God's demand for justice and righteousness, Hosea emphasized God's demand for faithfulness. Hosea challenges all of us to examine the level of our commitment to God.

Do we remain faithful to God even when other "lovers" tempt us? Do we look for satisfaction in other places? Do we give God a wholehearted, life-long commitment? Do we comprehend the awesome depth of God's love for each of us, personally? Or do we view our relationship with God as just one of the many friendships that we must maintain?

PERSONAL PRESCRIPTION
HOSEA AND YOU

 Give each student a copy of **Hosea and You** (page 37) then provide a quiet five minutes or so for them to think and write their way through it.

> ### RUNAWAY
> If you have time, and if it seems appropriate for your group, read Hosea 11:1-9 to your group. God loves us not only as a husband loves a wife, but also as a mother loves a child. Read **"The Runaway Bunny"** to your students. Or have it read by another respected adult (maybe a favorite Sunday school teacher) or just a good reader. (This has been done with great success in many senior high youth groups. The message is simple, profound, and relates perfectly to this lesson.)

PRAYER

Close with a prayer like this—

Dear God,
It's hard for us to comprehend how intensely you love us. We don't deserve
it. And we don't always respond to it the way we should. Forgive us for all
the times we've rejected you or left you. Help us learn how to be more
faithful to you. We want to know you and love you more and more each
day. Amen.

Famous Pairs

Below is an incomplete list of famous pairs. Fill in the missing half of each pair. (Extra points if you can identify where the pair comes from—TV show, movie, fairy tale, game, et cetera.)

Jack and—
Bert and—
Anthony and—
Scarlett O'Hara and—
Adam and—
Clark Kent and—
Romeo and—
Mike and—
Hansel and—
Calvin and—
Now and—
Dr. Jekyll and—
Ali Baba and—
Lewis and—
Peanut butter and—
Stars and—
Chutes and—
Sweet and—
Vinegar and—
Chip and—
Ben and—
Green Eggs and—

I Do, I Don't

Discussion Starter:

As a group, read Hosea 2:2-13. Then talk about the following, jotting down any insights, comments, or questions you may have.

What was God's reaction to Israel's unfaithfulness? Does this fit with your image of God? Talk about that.

Think of reasons why the Israelites might have followed other gods. Discuss these.

What things or "gods" compete with the true God for your attention and devotion? Talk about these.

Are you ever unfaithful to God? If so, talk about when, why, and the results.

The church today is often compared to Israel in the Old Testament. Do you think the church is faithful to God? Unfaithful? Talk about this.

Hosea and You
(personal prescription)

Think about the message of Hosea...

- I, God, love you with every fiber of my being.

- I am totally committed to you, no matter what.

- When you reject my love and walk away from me, my heart breaks with sorrow... and my soul burns with anger—and sorrow and pain.

- Why would you look anywhere else for the things only I can give you?

- Stay with me and see how precious life can be.

Think about yourself...

- What part of Hosea's message is speaking to you?

- What can you do to begin strengthening your commitment and faithfulness to God?

- Write a brief message to yourself below about those things. Be sure to think and pray about this issue during the week.

Imagine a marriage-like ceremony between you and God...

- What would you want to say to God in your vows? Write it here.

ISAIAH
(part 1)
The Political Prophet

PUNDITS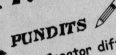

The Creator differed in character from his creation. The people, even Isaiah, were unclean.
Prophets and Poets, 35

For [Isaiah] the integrity, more, the very existence of his faith, was dependent upon the decision taken on political issues...he stood for political isolation, a rejection of all diplomatic alliances, because only that way could the distinctive character of his people's faith and worship witness to the uniquely personal character of their God.
Prophets and Poets, 33

The book of Isaiah is expansive, dealing with virtually everything that is involved in being a people of God on this planet Earth.
The Message, 12

There are frustrations in store for him who expects God to succeed at every turn in history.
The Prophets, 73

Isaiah's primary concern is not Judah's foreign policy, but rather the inner state of the nation.
The Prophets, 77

...[Isaiah] deals not with the anger, but with the sorrow of God.
The Prophets, 80

PROFILE
- Isaiah means "the Lord is Salvation"
- Received his calling in 742 B.C., the year King Uzziah died
- Message primarily to Southern Kingdom (Judah)
- An aristocratic and influential member of society
- Advisor to four of Judah's kings

PURPOSE OF PROPHETIC PRONOUNCEMENTS
TO UNVEIL AND COMMUNICATE THE FULL SCOPE OF GOD'S JUDGMENT AND SALVATION.

- God alone is holy.
- Hope is found in God alone.
- The establishment of God's kingdom on earth will be accomplished.

FROM OLD TO NEW
(where verses from this book are quoted in the New Testament)

Isaiah 6:3 ↔ Revelation 4:8
Isaiah 7:14 ↔ Matthew 1:23
Isaiah 8:17 ↔ Hebrews 2:13
Isaiah 11:10 ↔ Romans 15:12
Isaiah 25:8 ↔ 1 Corinthians 15:54
Isaiah 29:13 ↔ Mark 7:6-7
Isaiah 40:3-5 ↔ Luke 3:4-6

PREVIEW

Here was the political situation when Isaiah began to prophesy:
- The Northern Kingdom, Israel, was in dire straits and would soon be conquered by Assyria.
- Meanwhile, the Southern Kingdom, Judah—where Isaiah lived—was enjoying peace and prosperity.

Here was the spiritual situation when Isaiah began to prophesy:
- Israel had turned her back on God. God was using Assyria, a wicked nation, to punish his people.
- Judah, though politically more secure than Israel, wasn't much better off spiritually. Isaiah frequently warned the people to repent or face God's wrath and judgment.

Because Judah was a small nation, her kings were often tempted to form alliances with bigger nations as a means of protection. In such alliances, the smaller country was put in a position of keeping Big Brother happy—which often meant erecting temples for Big Brother's pagan gods and idols. Isaiah knew this would threaten his people's unique and distinctive faith. The promise of political protection wasn't worth the spiritual price.

One of Isaiah's primary messages was this—trust God for protection, not men.

Judah didn't listen. When King Hezekiah of Judah saw Assyria overrun next-door Israel (722 B.C.), he decided to throw in his lot with Egypt, hoping that the alliance would prevent Judah from suffering the same fate. When Assyria came knocking on Judah's door (701), only the capital city of Jerusalem managed to resist.

From then on, Isaiah's message included warnings about a new approaching enemy—Babylon.

PRECEPTS & PRINCIPLES 🖉

PRICELESS POETRY AND PROSE FROM ISAIAH

In the last days the mountain of the Lord's temple will be established as chief among the mountains; it will be raised above the hills, and all nations will stream to it. Many peoples will come and say, "Come, let us go up to the mountain of the Lord, to the house of the God of Jacob. He will teach us his ways, so that we may walk in his paths." (Isaiah 2:2-3)

Woe to those who call evil good and good evil, who put darkness for light and light for darkness, who put bitter for sweet and sweet for bitter. (4:20)

"Holy, holy, holy is the Lord Almighty; the whole earth is full of his glory." (6:3)

Yet the Lord longs to be gracious to you; he rises to show you compassion. For the Lord is a God of justice. Blessed are all who wait for him! (30:18)

PLAY
WHOSE KING IS IT, ANYWAY?

Before the lesson, photocopy the page of slips for **Whose King Is It, Anyway?** (page 45) and cut them apart. Add some kings of your own to the blank slips if you want. Divide students into groups of four or five. Give one slip to each group and instruct them to take a few minutes to write a short, creative description of their king—a riddle, limerick, a simple list of characteristics, anything. When they're finished, each group will read their description to the entire group, which will try to guess the king's identity.

PAUSE

Segue from the game into the Bible-study part of the lesson by saying something like:

In today's world, we're more familiar with prime ministers and presidents than with kings. Isaiah lived in a time when a king's personality and morality defined the nation. God spoke through Isaiah both to the nation of Judah as a whole and to the kings as individuals.

PONDER POINT - *option 1*
THE KINGS

Divide your students into five groups. Give each group a copy of **The King and I** (page 46) and assign one king to each group. Give them up to 10 minutes to work on the handouts, and then regather. Have someone from each small group offer a short bio of his or her group's king. Then say something like—

Isaiah was a prophet for more than 60 years. During that time, Judah had many different kings, each with a unique personality, leadership style, strengths, and weaknesses. Sometimes they were receptive to Isaiah's messages, sometimes they ignored them, and sometimes they defiantly rejected them. Isaiah was never sure what to expect from Judah's rulers. But there was one King he could always count on—the Lord. Isaiah wrote one of the greatest descriptions of God in the Bible.

Have someone read Isaiah 6:1-4. You might want to have the entire group read verse 3 in unison. Have another student read Revelation 4:1-8. Then give each student a copy of **The Holiness of God** (page 47) to read silently.

OF WIZARDS AND WACKOS

For yet another look at some less-than-spectacular rulers, show the clip from **"The Wizard of Oz"** in which Dorothy and her friends discover that the great and terrible wizard is only an old man behind a curtain. (1:27:22—1:29:13) Or one of the several clips from **"Monty Python and the Holy Grail"** in which King Arthur is depicted as a doofus. (4:00—6:53)

Here's the quote they'll read in that handout:

> "Holy is the way God is. To be holy he does not conform to a standard. He is that standard. Because he is holy, his attributes [or characteristics] are holy; that is, whatever we think of as belonging to God must be thought of as holy. God is holy and he has made holiness the moral condition necessary to the health of his universe. Whatever is holy is healthy; evil is a moral sickness that must end ultimately in death. The English word *holy* comes from the Anglo-Saxon *halig, hal,* meaning *well, whole.* Since God's first concern for his universe is its moral health, that is, its holiness, whatever is contrary to this is necessarily under his eternal displeasure. To preserve his creation God must destroy whatever would destroy it. Every wrathful judgment in the history of the world has been a holy act of preservation."
> (*The Knowledge of the Holy*, A.W. Tozer)

After the students have finished reading, gather and discuss the following:

- *How would you define holiness? Does Isaiah's experience and the description you just read change your understanding of holiness? Talk about this.*
- *People use the word holy in everyday speech as an expression of surprise or shock (e.g., "Holy cow!"). What do you think of this practice?*
- *Why do you think Isaiah was so concerned with God's holiness?*
- *Do you spend time thinking about or focusing on God's holiness? When and how do you do this?*
- *How important do you think it is for Christians to acknowledge and understand God's holiness? Why?*

PONDER POINT - option 2
THE MAN

> "The sudden realization of his personal depravity came like a stroke from heaven upon the trembling heart of Isaiah at the moment when he had his revolutionary vision of the holiness of God. His pain-filled cry, 'Woe is me! For I am undone, because I am a man of unclean lips, and I dwell in the midst of a people of unclean lips: for mine eyes have seen the King, the Lord of hosts,' expresses the feeling of every man who has discovered himself under his disguises and has been confronted with an inward sight of the holy whiteness that is God. Such as experience cannot but be emotionally violent." (*The Knowledge of the Holy*, 162)

People spend a lot of time comparing themselves to others. Teens especially are subtly encouraged to measure their worth by noting whether they're as skinny, beautiful, well-dressed, popular, or athletic as so-and-so. Those who feel they'll never measure up to the world's standards—which are false images of perfection—are left feeling depressed, dejected, worthless, and hopeless.

When Isaiah sees God and measures himself against the true standard of holiness, he sees himself as he really is—a sinner, totally unworthy. Unlike many of today's teens, Isaiah measures himself against a *true* image of perfection—the Holy God. His response isn't one of depressed and deject-ed *feelings*. Instead, it's an obvious acknowledgement of the *truth*.

Read Isaiah 6:1-5 to your students. Give each a copy of **Reality Exposed** (page 48). Let them have several minutes to work on this alone.

After your students have read and thought about the handout, discuss the following in either small groups or all together—

- *When Isaiah saw God (or met him, at any rate), why do you think the prophet's immediate response was to recognize his sinfulness, impurity, and uncleanness? Talk about that.*
- *What effect do you think Isaiah's response ("Woe is me!") had on his job as prophet?*
- *What do you think the angel's response ("Your guilt is taken away and your sin atoned for") had on Isaiah's job as prophet?*
- *Why might it have been important for Isaiah to be aware of both his unclean and forgiven self? Do you think this is important for us today? Why? Do you think these two should be focused on equally? One more than the other? Why?*

PONDER POINT - *option 3*

THE QUESTION

Once Isaiah sees God, acknowledges the Lord's holiness, recognizes and admits his own sinfulness, and is purified, he's ready for duty. Interestingly enough, God doesn't give Isaiah a job right away. He first poses this question:

"Whom shall I send? And who will go for us?"

Imagine standing before the Holy God of the universe and hearing those words. How would you feel? Answering questions can be terrifying. *What if I give the wrong answer? What if someone laughs at me? What if my voice cracks? Can I phone a friend?* And this is just when the questions are posed by teachers, parents, friends, and other humans. How much more terrifying might it be when the question is posed by God? *What if I'm not qualified? What if I screw things up? What if someone laughs at me?*

And worst of all—*If I say yes, will God make me go someplace horrible to live with people I can't stand doing a job I detest?*

Let's be honest. If someone asked us, "Who shall I send and who will go for me?" wouldn't most of us answer with something like, "Well, that all depends on where you want me to go!"

On a whiteboard, make three columns. Label them with these phrases:

- PLACES I'M AFRAID GOD MIGHT SEND ME
- THINGS I'M AFRAID GOD MIGHT WANT ME TO DO
- STUFF I'M AFRAID GOD MIGHT WANT ME TO GIVE UP

Say something like—

God wants us to give ourselves to him totally. He doesn't want just a part of us. He wants all of us. That scares some people because they think God's the kind of guy who likes to make people miserable. Yet Isaiah said "yes" to God before he even knew what the task was. Do you trust God enough to do the same?

Have students brainstorm with you about some of their worries or fears regarding God's expectations. List their ideas in the appropriate columns on the whiteboard. Some examples:

- *Places I'm afraid God will send me:* secluded jungle, dangerous part of the city
- *Things I'm afraid God might want me to do:* be a missionary, stay single
- *Stuff I'm afraid God might want me to give up:* dream of becoming a doctor, involvement with music/sports/other hobby

Generally these fears are based on misconceptions of God—but that doesn't make these fears any less real. Rather than telling kids to simply stop being afraid, try to clear up their misconceptions by presenting the truth. Have volunteers read the following verses to the group:

Psalm 138:8	John 10:10	Colossians 3:12-14
Psalm 139:13-16	Galatians 4:6-7	Hebrews 13:20-21
Philippians 1:3-6	Ephesians 2:10	1 Peter 2:9
Romans 8:28	Ephesians 5:8-10	1 John 4:4
Romans 8:37-39	Philippians 4:12-13	1 John 4:15-18

PAUSE

Segue into the next section, Personal Prescription, by saying something like this:

Isaiah's encounter with God teaches us these things:

1. The first step in having a relationship with God is recognizing him for who he is—the one and only holy God.

2. The second step is to recognize ourselves for who we are—unclean human beings who cannot stand in the presence of a holy God.

3. The third step is to let God make us clean by purifying us from our sins.

4. The fourth step is to give ourselves totally to God, to say "yes" to whatever he asks us to do. This gets easier the more we get to know him and the more we trust him.

PERSONAL PRESCRIPTION

Hand out copies of **Why It's Hard to Say YES, and How to Get Over It** (page 49), divide your students into small groups of four or five, and let them explore the questions.

WHOSE KING IS IT, ANYWAY?

Slips for the activity Whose King Is It, Anyway? in the Isaiah (part 1) lesson. Photocopy this page, cut apart, and distribute at the appropriate point in the lesson.

••

Old King Cole (nursery rhyme)

••

King Arthur

••

King Triton (from The Little Mermaid)

••

King Kong

••

Martin Luther King, Jr.

••

Chicken a la King

••

King of the Jungle

••

Larry King ("Larry King Live")

••

Kings in the Corner (card game)

••

King of the Hill (TV Show)

••

••

••

••

••

••

The King and I

Isaiah prophesied from the end of Uzziah's reign into Manasseh's reign. Read about one of the kings listed below to find out what kind of man and ruler he was.

Name the King & part of the Bible	King was famous for
Uzziah (2 Chronicles 26:1-22)	Made a king at 16
Jotham (2 Chronicles 27:1-9)	Conquered the Ammonites
Ahaz (2 Chronicles 28:1-26)	Worshiped idols
Hezekiah (2 Chronicles 29:1-11, 30:1-5, 31:1-10, 31:20-32:8, 32:24-33)	Ruled for 29 years
Manasseh (2 Chronicles 33:1-20)	Practiced sorcery, divination and witchcraft

List some facts/descriptions about your group's king. (What kind of person was he? How did he treat the people? What did he think of God? Did he worship idols?)

Name of your King	King was famous for

The Holiness of God

An excerpt from *The Knowledge of the Holy*, A.W. Tozer

"Holy is the way God is. To be holy he does not conform to a standard. He is that standard. Because he is holy, his attributes [characteristics] are holy; that is, whatever we think of as belonging to God must be thought of as holy. God is holy and he has made holiness the moral condition necessary to the health of his universe. Whatever is holy is healthy; evil is a moral sickness that must end ultimately in death. The English word holy comes from the Anglo-Saxon *halig, hal,* meaning "well, whole." Since God's first concern for his universe is its moral health, that is, its holiness, whatever is contrary to this is necessarily under his eternal displeasure. To preserve his creation God must destroy whatever would destroy it. Every wrathful judgment in the history of the world has been a holy act of preservation."

Reality Exposed

You are already clean because of the word I have spoken to you. (John 15:3)

You are already clean because of the word I have spoken to you. (John 15:3)

If we confess our sins, he is faithful and just and will forgive us our sins and purify us from all unrighteousness. (1 John 1:9)

Who may ascend the hill of the Lord? Who may stand in his holy place? He who has clean hands and a pure heart. (Psalm 24:3, 4)

Let us draw near to God with a sincere heart in full assurance of faith, having our hearts sprinkled to cleanse us from a guilty conscience and having our bodies washed with pure water. (Hebrews 10:22)

(Jesus Christ) gave himself for us to redeem us from all wickedness and to purify for himself a people that are his very own, eager to do what is good. (Titus 2:14)

Cleanse me with hyssop, and I will be clean; wash me, and I will be whiter than snow. (Psalm 51:7)

May he strengthen your hearts so that you will be blameless and holy in the presence of our God and Father when our Lord Jesus comes with all his holy ones. (1 Thessalonians 3:13)

He will keep you strong to the end, so that you will be blameless on the day of our Lord Jesus Christ. (1 Corinthians 1:8)

For he chose us in him before the creation of the world to be holy and blameless in his sight. In him we have redemption through his blood, the forgiveness of sins, in accordance with the riches of God's grace that he lavished on us with all wisdom and understanding. (Ephesians 1:4, 7)

May God himself, the God of peace, sanctify you through and through. May your whole spirit, soul and body be kept blameless at the coming of our Lord Jesus Christ. The one who calls you is faithful and he will do it. (1 Thessalonians 5:23, 24)

Take a minute to think about God's holiness...

"Woe to me! I am ruined! For I am a man of unclean lips." —Isaiah

"See, this has touched your lips; your guilt is taken away and your sin atoned for." —Angel, to Isaiah

"Christ was sacrificed once to take away the sins of many people; we have been made holy through the sacrifice of the body of Jesus Christ once for all."—the writer of the letter to the Hebrews

Take a minute to think about yourself before you began a relationship with Christ. Describe yourself then (whether it was years, months, or weeks ago) by completing this thought:

Woe to me, for I am a person_____

_____

_____

_____

Take a minute to think about yourself now, as a forgiven child of God. Complete this thought:

Because Jesus died and paid the penalty for my sins,
I am a person_____

_____

_____

Why It's Hard to Say YES, and How to Get Over it
(personal prescription)

In your small group, talk about some of these issues.

What things might be keeping you from saying yes to whatever it is God is asking you to do?

- Peer pressure?
- The world's influence?
- Personal insecurity?
- Something else?

Talk about how you can begin focusing on God's holiness more and these other things less.

By yourself, privately...

Write here one thing you sense God is asking you to do. It might be as simple as, "Will you show more kindness to your sister?" Or maybe it's something like, "Will you consider giving up a month of your summer vacation to do a short-term mission project?"

If you haven't sensed God asking you anything specific, take a few minutes to read Philippians 2:1-18.

Consider this...

God is calling each one of us, at this very moment, to do something for him. What is it? Simply this—love God and love others. Will you say "yes" to him?

And one more thing...

"The important thing is that he expects you to trust him, above all else. He expects you to love him and to serve him to the best of your knowledge and ability, but the main thing is that he expects you to believe in the fact that he loves you. Not only to believe that he loves you, but to act as if you believed it. Very few people have been able to love and serve God perfectly, and you are no exception. You are not expected to love and serve him perfectly. As a matter of fact, by yourself you can't even begin to do it. But that isn't necessary: all that is required is that you have the willingness to do it, admit that it's beyond your powers, and ask him to help you to do it. You must want to do it, and have enough faith in his love for you as to believe that he can and will enable you to do it." (from *Me, Myself and You* by Vincent P. Collins)

ISAIAH
(part 2) His Message

PUNDITS

What is the issue that haunts this prophet's soul?...How marvelous is the world that God has created, and how horrible is the world that man has made.

The Prophets, 78

Ahaz decided that it was more expedient to be son and servant to the king of Assyria than son and servant to the invisible God. He took refuge in a lie.

The Prophets, 65

Those who act as if there were no God, no divine order in history, are more foolish than one who would sow and plant, while completely disregarding the nature of the soil or the seasons of the year. They act as if man were alone, as if their deeds were carried out in the dark, as if there were no God Who saw, no God Who knew.

The Prophets, 70

PROFILE

- Either wrote entire book bearing his name, or wrote only chapters 1 to 39 (there's considerable disagreement about this among scholars)

- Most educated of all the prophets

- Considered the most eloquent and literary of all biblical writers

- Quoted in the New Testament more than all other prophets combined

- According to tradition, was sawn in half by order of King Manasseh

PURPOSE OF PROPHETIC PRONOUNCEMENTS

TO DELIVER MESSAGES OF WARNING, JUDGMENT, COMFORT, DELIVERANCE, AND HOPE TO GOD'S PEOPLE, BOTH FOR THE PRESENT AND FUTURE.

PREVIEW

A PEEK AT THE PITH OF ISAIAH, CHAPTERS 40-66

Isaiah can be divided into three main sections—chapters 1-39, 40-55, and 56-66. The first section was written with an eye on Assyria, a neighboring enemy at the time Isaiah was writing. The second and third sections were written with an eye on a future enemy, Babylon.

In the first section (chapters 1-39) Isaiah encourages his people to amend their wicked ways and return to God. They had turned to idol worship, grown lazy and proud in their prosperity, and rejected God's leadership. Isaiah also warns his listeners about the danger of making alliances with foreign nations.

FROM OLD TO NEW
(where verses from this book are quoted in the New Testament)

Isaiah 40:6-8 ↔ 1 Peter 1:24-25
Isaiah 49:6 ↔ Acts 13:47
Isaiah 52:11 ↔ 2 Corinthians 6:17
Isaiah 53:1 ↔ John 12:38
Isaiah 54:1 ↔ Galatians 4:27
Isaiah 65:17 ↔ 2 Peter 3:13

The second section (chapters 40-55) contains the well-known "Servant Songs" that point toward the promise of a coming Messiah.

Some scholars view Isaiah as a Bible within a Bible. The 39 chapters in the first section reflect the 39 chapters of the Old Testament, proclaiming judgment on a stubborn and defiant people. The 26 chapters of the second and third sections parallel the 26 New Testament chapters, delivering messages of grace, hope, comfort, and the promise of new life.

PRECEPTS & PRINCIPLES

PRICELESS POETRY AND PROSE FROM ISAIAH

And the glory of the Lord will be revealed, and all mankind together will see it. For the mouth of the Lord has spoken. (Isaiah 40:5)

The grass withers and the flowers fall, but the word of our God stands forever. (40:8)

Do you not know? Have you not heard? The Lord is the everlasting God, the Creator of the ends of the earth. He will not grow tired or weary, and his understanding no one can fathom. He gives strength to the weary and increases the power of the weak. Even youths grow tired and weary, and young men stumble and fall; but those who hope in the Lord will renew their strength. They will soar on wings like eagles; they will run and not grow weary, they will walk and not be faint. (40:28-31)

It is too small a thing for you to be my servant to restore the tribes of Jacob and bring back those of Israel I have kept. I will also make you a light for the Gentiles, that you may bring my salvation to the ends of the earth. (49:6)

PLAY

Before the lesson, mark out three different sections in the room using chairs, tape, or cones. Label the three different sections— UR/MESOPOTAMIA/ASSYRIA; CANAAN/ISRAEL/JUDAH; and EGYPT. Make Israel/Judah the middle section. In each section put a pile of clothing—hat, shirt, jacket, boots, mittens, et cetera. Choose individual students to represent Abraham, Joseph, Moses, the King of Assyria, the King of Egypt, and the King of Judah. Encourage the students to move *quickly* from section to section. They must wear some of the clothing of whatever section they're in until instructed otherwise.

All set? Now walk your students through a short visual history:

1. **Abraham lived in Ur** *[put on clothes]*.
2. **God tells Abraham to go to Canaan** *[add Canaan's clothes]*.
3. **God makes a covenant with Abraham and tells him to worship God exclusively** *[remove Ur clothes]*.
4. **A few generations later, along comes Joseph** *[Joseph takes Abraham's place and clothes]*.
5. **Joseph is sent to Egypt by his bad brothers where he works for Pharaoh** *[add Egyptian clothes]*.

6. A few generations later, along comes Moses *[Moses takes Joseph's place and clothes]*.
7. God tells Moses to go to the Promised Land *[put on Canaan clothes]*.
8. God tells Moses to worship only God *[remove Egypt clothes]*.
9. A few generations later, along come some kings from Assyria, Judah, and Egypt *[Kings go to their section and put on clothes.]*
10. God keeps reminding the Kings of Judah to worship only God, to wear only his clothes.
11. When the Kings of Judah think the Assyrians want to hurt them, they make friends with the Egyptians. The Egyptians make them wear their clothes *[Put on Egyptian clothes]*.
12. When the Kings of Judah think the Egyptians want to hurt them, they make friends with the Assyrians. The Assyrians make them take off the Egyptian clothes and put on their clothes *[Take off Egypt clothes, put on Assyrian clothes]*.
13. Some of the Kings of Judah think the Egyptian clothes are really cool, so they decide to keep the Egyptian clothes on anyway *[Put Egyptian clothes back on]*.
14. God says, "Look at you. You're a fashion mess. You are the worst dressed person on the earth. Haven't I told you before never to mix plaids with stripes, reds with pinks? I can't stand looking at you."
15. The end.

PAUSE

Segue from the dress-up game to the Bible-study part of the lesson by saying something like:

FOR A MORE VISUAL EFFECT...

Choose bright, ugly, loud clothes for Assyria and Egypt, and normal clothes for Judah. When you get to step 14, you can add some more on and off steps just for fun: "God told the King to take off those ugly Assyrian clothes...the King decided to put the funky Assyrian pants back on...God told the King to take off those obnoxious Egyptian clothes...the King liked the Egyptian clothes better than the Judah clothes, and since he was overheating from all the layers, he took off the Judah clothes and put the Egyptian ones back on..." You get the idea.

It's easy to see what happens when a person (or nation) tries to keep too many people happy. Things get chaotic and confusing. Life is like that—if we continue to build relationships that require us to make compromises in order to keep other people happy, we'll begin to forget who we really are and what we really believe.

PONDER POINT - option 1
MISPLACED TRUST

Judah (Isaiah's home) was a small country. It was often the target of larger countries that were in the business of conquering and swallowing up the little guys. On several occasions Judah formed alliances with other nations as a means of protection. But God took a firm stand against this, and he used Isaiah to communicate his message.

Have different students or leaders read the following passages to the group:

• **Isaiah 7:1-9 (lots of weird names—you might want to read this one yourself or write out a paraphrase)**
• **Isaiah 20:1-6**

- **Isaiah 30:1-5**
- **Isaiah 31:1**
- **Isaiah 33:22**

Talk about these things with your students—

- *Why do you think God didn't want his people to form alliances with other nations?*
- *Why do you think the kings of Judah ignored God's instruction about this?*
- *Imagine that the church is God's present-day country filled with his chosen people. Do you think the same warning holds true today? If so, what alliances do Christians need to avoid?*
- *Judah often put her trust in humankind—that is, other nations—instead of God. Do you ever do that? Talk about situations, places, and times in your life when it's tempting to rely on humans instead of God.*
- *Judah's relationship with God was watered down and eventually destroyed as a result of her alliances. Do you see a parallel for us today? What things might cause our faith to become weak and watered down?*

You might want to keep a list of Christians' "dangerous allies" that are mentioned in the discussion.

PONDER POINT - option 2
THE SUFFERING SERVANT

Chapters 40 to 55 of Isaiah contain the four well-known "Servant Songs" (42:1-4, 49:1-6, 50:4-9, 52:13-53:12). These have been interpreted as descriptions of all sorts of things: 1) of the prophet himself, 2) of the nation of Israel, 3) of the coming Messiah, 4) of the present day church, and 5) of a combination of these things.

Some scholars have called the Servant Song in Isaiah 52:13 – 53:12 "The Gospel of the Old Testament." Divide your students into groups. Have them read this Song together, and then work on the **Suffering Servant** handout (page 56).

When the groups have finished, regather together and discuss the handout. Many characteristics of the "suffering servant" are attributed to Christ in the gospels. Here are some related Scriptures you might want to share with your students:

- **Romans 8:31-34**
- **Ephesians 1:7**
- **Philippians 2:5-11**
- **Hebrews 5:7-9, 7:25, 9:26-28**
- **1 Peter 2:24-25**
- **1 John 3:4-5**

You may want to conclude this activity with words to this effect:

Of all the religions in the world, Christianity is unique in that we have a God—Jesus Christ—who reaches out to us, who suffered for us, who did the hard work for us, who served us so that we can serve him. He is totally opposite from every other so-called god. Talk about the importance of that. What does it mean to you that the God you know personally suffered for you?

PONDER POINT - option 3
GOOD NEWS

"The unconditional promises of Second Isaiah [chapters 40-55] tend to become dependant on right behavior in Third Isaiah [56-66]; hopes that are for all in Isaiah 40-55 are generally reserved for a narrower group of faithful in chapters 56-66." (*Prophets and Poets*, 81)

It's true that Jesus, the Suffering Servant, died for the sins of everyone. It's also true, however, that not everyone chooses to follow Jesus. The opportunity for forgiveness and new life through Christ is universal. But the acceptance of it by humans is limited. Unlike Isaiah, not everyone says yes when God asks, "Will you follow me?"

The last 10 chapters of Isaiah explain what God desires and expects from those who would follow him. Give a copy of **Good News** (page 57) to each student. Let them work in small groups, pairs, or individually.

The questions are:

- *What does it mean to commit yourself to the Lord? Have you ever done this?*
- *How would you define a humble spirit? Is humility something a person has, something a person learns, or something else entirely?*
- *Repentance involves turning and changing direction, not just feeling sorry for something you've said or done. Have you ever made a decision to turn and change direction in your life? What (or who) did you turn from? What (or who) did you turn toward?*
- *We all begin life with our backs turned to God—sinners. Becoming a Christian involves turning our face toward God (repentance) and receiving his forgiveness. If a person faces God, what things would you expect to see in that person's life?*

This is what God wants your life to be like. Will you let him do this for you?

PERSONAL PRESCRIPTION
ISAIAH AND YOU

Give everyone a copy of **Isaiah and You** (page 58). Have each person decide which of the three Ponder Points is the most challenging for them (putting their trust in God instead of people...getting to know Jesus as the one true God who personally suffered for every individual...living a genuine life of faith face-to-face with God). Students can do this activity alone, or you can have them divide into three groups based on the Ponder Points.

Suffering Servant

Read Isaiah 52:13-53:12 together in your small group.

52:

13 See, my servant will act wisely; he will be raised and lifted up and highly exalted.

14 Just as there were many who were appalled at him—his appearance was so disfigured beyond that of any man and his form marred beyond human likeness—

15 So will he sprinkle many nations, and kings will shut their mouths because of him. For what they were not told, they will see, and what they have not heard, they will understand.

53:

1 Who has believed our message and to whom has the arm of the LORD been revealed?

2 He grew up before him like a tender shoot, and like a root out of dry ground. He had no beauty or majesty to attract us to him, nothing in his appearance that we should desire him.

3 He was despised and rejected by men, a man of sorrows, and familiar with suffering. Like one from whom men hide their faces he was despised, and we esteemed him not.

4 Surely he took up our infirmities and carried our sorrows, yet we considered him stricken by God, smitten by him, and afflicted.

5 But he was pierced for our transgressions, he was crushed for our iniquities; the punishment that brought us peace was upon him, and by his wounds we are healed.

6 We all, like sheep, have gone astray, each of us has turned to his own way; and the LORD has laid on him the iniquity of us all.

7 He was oppressed and afflicted, yet he did not open his mouth; he was led like a lamb to the slaughter, and as a sheep before her shearers is silent, so he did not open his mouth.

8 By oppression and judgment he was taken away. And who can speak of his descendants? For he was cut off from the land of the living; for the transgression of my people he was stricken.

9 He was assigned a grave with the wicked, and with the rich in his death, though he had done no violence, nor was any deceit in his mouth.

10 Yet it was the LORD's will to crush him and cause him to suffer, and though the LORD makes his life a guilt offering, he will see his offspring and prolong his days, and the will of the LORD will prosper in his hand.

11 After the suffering of his soul, he will see the light [of life] and be satisfied; by his knowledge my righteous servant will justify many, and he will bear their iniquities.

12 Therefore I will give him a portion among the great, and he will divide the spoils with the strong, because he poured out his life unto death, and was numbered with the transgressors. For he bore the sin of many, and made intercession for the transgressors.

 Did Jesus fulfill Isaiah's prophecies about the coming Messiah? Below, try to fill every line under "Jesus" that corresponds with the characteristics under "The Suffering Servant." See the first example. (Note the Scripture reference if possible).

The Suffering Servant	Jesus
acts wisely (52:13)	youth Jesus teaching in the temple (Luke 2:41-47)
will be exalted (52:13)	
will reveal God's power (53:1)	
will come from humble beginnings (53:2)	
won't look or act like a king (53:2)	
will be rejected by many people (53:3)	
will suffer (53:3)	
won't be recognized for who he truly is (53:3)	
will experience human sorrows (53:4)	
will be persecuted for the sins of others (53:5)	
will provide peace and healing through his suffering (53:5)	
won't try to talk his way out of things (53:7)	
will be accused and judged unfairly (53:8)	
will die before having any descendants (53:8)	
will die with criminals (53:9)	
will be buried with the rich (53:9)	
will live a sinless life (53:9)	
will die as part of God's plan (53:10)	
will have offspring and descendants as a result of his death (53:10)	
will do God's work willingly (53:10)	
will come back to life (53:11)	
will make it possible for people to be acquitted (53:12)	
will be rewarded by God like a victorious king (53:12)	
will bear the burden of the world's sins (53:12)	
will plead (intercede) to God on behalf of sinners (53:12)	

Good News

Read these verses from Isaiah. Take special note of the italicized words, which describe a person's relationship with God—what it is, how to have it, how to live it. After each verse, there's a question for you to think about. (These verses are taken from the New Living Translation.)

"And my blessings are for Gentiles, too, when they *commit* themselves to the Lord" (Isaiah 56:3).

What does it mean to commit yourself to the Lord? Have you ever done this?

"The high and lofty one who inhabits eternity, the Holy One, says this: 'I live in that high and holy place with those whose spirits are contrite and *humble*. I refresh the humble and give new courage to those with *repentant* hearts.'" (57:15).

How would you define a humble spirit? Is humility something a person has, something a person learns, or something else entirely?

Repentance involves turning and changing direction, not just feeling sorry for something you've said or done. Have you ever made a decision to turn and change direction in your life? What (or who) did you turn from? What (or who) did you turn toward?

"Listen! The Lord is not too weak to save you, and he is not becoming deaf. *He can hear you when you call.* But there is a problem—your sins have cut you off from God. Because of your sin, he has turned away and will not listen anymore" (59:1-2).

"For our sins are piled up before God and testify against us. Yes, we know what sinners we are. We know that we have *rebelled* against the Lord. We have turned our backs on God" (59:12-13).

"'The Redeemer will come to Jerusalem,' says the Lord, 'to buy back those in Israel who have *turned from their sins.* And this is my covenant with them,' says the Lord. 'My Spirit will not leave them, and neither will these words I have give you.'" (59:20-21).

We all begin life with our backs turned to God—sinners. Becoming a Christian involves turning our face toward God (repentance) and receiving his forgiveness. If a person faces God, what things would you expect to see in that person's life?

"The Lord will guide you continually, watering your life when you are dry and keeping you healthy, too. You will be like a *well-watered garden,* like an everflowing spring" (58:11).

This is what God wants your life to be like. Will you let him do this for you?

Isaiah and You
(personal prescription)

From the list below, choose what is most challenging for you or what you'd like to work on most. Then explore the corresponding question.

Putting my trust in God, not in people.

Think of all God did when he rescued the Israelites from Egypt—the plagues, the Passover, parting the Red Sea, manna from heaven, fresh water in the wilderness…the list is long—and brought them to the Promised Land. Imagine how God felt when, hundred of years later, the Israelites wanted to make an alliance with Egypt, the very people God had rescued them from.

Are there any things or people in your life that God has worked hard to "rescue" you from that you still turn to for comfort (or help or fun) now and then? Think of how that might make God feel. Then think of some ways you can begin to change that tendency.

Getting to know Jesus as the one true God who personally suffered for me.

If you've never read one of the Gospels (Matthew, Mark, Luke, or John) from beginning to end, do it this week. Mark is a good one to start with. It's short and fast-paced. Keep a list of all the examples of Jesus being ridiculed, rejected, ignored, denied, or persecuted.

Imagine that you made a costly and painful sacrifice for someone you truly love—maybe a friend or family member. What if that person never spent time with you or tried to build on the relationship? What if they just blew off your sacrifice as something insignificant? What if they completely ignored your actions? Have you been doing that to Jesus, the suffering servant? If so, what will you do differently?

Living a genuine life of faith, face-to-face with God.

Imagine what it would be like if, on your wedding day, your new husband or wife looked at you after the ceremony and said, "Well, see ya 'round. Gotta go."

When two people commit to a marriage, it involves so much more than saying, "I do." It means living together, spending time together, getting to know one another, serving one another, making certain changes for the good of the relationship.

When a person says yes to a relationship with God, the same thing has to happen. You can't just say, "Well, see ya 'round. Gotta go." You need to start developing a genuine life of faith—and that requires at least as much hard work and commitment as a marriage does.

What things are you willing to begin doing to hold up your end of the relationship with God?

HABAKKUK
"Is That Your Final Answer?"
(Or, a Dialogue with God)

PUNDITS 🖉

I would say to all who decide to study and teach this book, we simply need to get out of God's way and let him communicate how meaningful it really is.

Living Insights Study Bible,
introduction to Habakkuk, 961

...in the first two chapters of Habakkuk we have prominently displayed for us another role of the prophet—that of asking the very difficult question—of asking God the very difficult questions, and then with single focus waiting and watching for the answer.

Storyteller's Companion, 184

...we are drawn to this book of the Old Testament, not because it gives us answers, but because it asks our questions.

Storyteller's Companion, 184

Christians sometimes talk as though it were blasphemous or improper to raise questions like [Habakkuk's]...the Old Testament is more robust and believes that if God is really God, he is quite capable of facing the most demanding questions we may put to him.

Prophets and Poets, 266

...in Habakkuk, as in other parts of the Bible, to have faith means to believe God's promise and to act as if it is going to be fulfilled...faith means living in the light of that which God has promised [the coming kingdom] and trusting that God will keep his promise.

Preaching from the Minor Prophets, 91

A startled, tormented man is Habakkuk.

The Prophets, 140

The world may be dismal; the wrath may turn the gardens into a desert; yet the prophet "will rejoice in the Lord."

The Prophets, 144

PROFILE

• Prophesied some-
time between 609
and 598 B.C.

• Was a contemporary
of Jeremiah

• Prophesied immediate-
ly after good King Josiah's
reign, during the time when
King Jehoikim reversed all
of Josiah's reforms, and
immediately before a devas-
tating Babylonian invasion

• The Dead Sea Scrolls
contain a full commentary
on chapters 1 and 2 of Habakkuk

• The only minor prophet who
never spoke directly to the people

• Is his name (and the book) pronounced ha-BAK-uk or HAB-a-kuk?
The world may never know...

FROM OLD TO NEW
(where verses from this book are quoted
in the New Testament)

Habakkuk 1:3 ↔ Acts 13:41
Habakkuk 2:3-4 ↔ Hebrews 10:37-38
Habakkuk 2:4 ↔ Romans 1:17 Galatians 3:11

Habakkuk started out exactly where we start out with our puzzled complaints and God-accusations, but he didn't stay there. He ended up in a world, along with us, where every detail in our lives of love for God is worked into something good.

The Message, introduction to Habakkuk, 533

PURPOSE OF PROPHETIC PRONOUNCEMENTS
TO REASSURE THE PEOPLE THAT EVIL WILL NOT LAST FOREVER AND THAT GOD IS IN CONTROL.

- God can handle our questions.
- God welcomes our questions.
- The only way to hear God's response is to wait patiently and quietly.
- God is in control of the universe.
- God always responds, but he doesn't always answer.

PREVIEW
A PEEK AT THE PITH OF HABAKKUK

Habakkuk lived in dark times. Good king Josiah had recently died, along with all of his spiritual reforms. The new king, Jehoiakim II, was nothing more than a puppet king for Egypt. He totally reversed all the reforms of Josiah. His reign was unjust and violent, characterized by forced labor, idolatry, and prophet persecution. As if things at home in Judah weren't bad enough, Habakkuk was also aware of Babylon's power and domination of all the surrounding countries. Babylon was ruthless, evil, powerful, and destructive.

And so begins Habakkuk's dialogue with God. He complains to God about current affairs and asks his first question: How long must we wait? When are you going to help us, God?

God answers: I'm on my way. I'm going to use the Babylonians to accomplish my purposes.

Habakkuk responds: The Babylonians?! Those wicked, evil pagans?! Are you crazy?! Apparently so. But you're also God. So I'll sit here quietly, watching and waiting for your explanation.

In time, God replies: Hey, I can use whomever I want to do whatever I want. But don't worry. Babylon will not escape judgment. Evil will not control the world. In the end, justice will be administered fairly.

Because he was watching and waiting, Habakkuk heard God's reply. Though God's ways are not explained, his sovereignty and love are reaffirmed. Habakkuk sings a song of praise to God's power, love, and overwhelming majesty.

PRECEPTS & PRINCIPLES
PRICELESS POETRY AND PROSE FROM HABAKKUK

I will stand at my watch and station myself on the ramparts; I will look to see what he will say to me, and what answer I am to give to this complaint (Habakkuk 2:1).

But the Lord is in his holy temple; let all the earth be silent before him (2:20).

Lord, I have heard of your fame; I stand in awe of your deeds, O Lord. Renew them in our day, in our time make them known; in wrath remember mercy (3:2).

The Sovereign Lord is my strength; he makes my feet like the feet of a deer, he enables me to go on the heights (3:19).

PLAY
IS THAT YOUR FINAL ANSWER?

Before the lesson, photocopy the page of slips on page 65 for **Is That Your Final Answer?** and cut them apart. Divide students into 12 groups. Give each group one of the slips. All of the dates commemorate actual events, but it's the students' job to come up with their own event for that date. (For example, they might decide that May 22, 1967, was the day that Betty Crocker finally perfected the boxed brownie mix.) Give them only one or two minutes to create their answers, write them on the back of the slips, and turn them in. When you've gathered all the slips, tell the students that you're going to read two answers for each date, the real one and a made-up one—and they'll get to vote on which they think it is.

> Keep the cards and the answer sheet behind a binder or folder so the group can't tell which one you're reading. Before the voting, read only the main title of the correct answer. Then, after the voting, read the details.

Dates & the Actual Events Connected to Them
(info from *Chase's*, 1998)

January 1, 1990 - December 31, 1999: Decade of the Brain
To raise public awareness of brain research. Public Law 101-58 established the 1990s decade as Decade of the Brain. A Presidential Proclamation, #6158, said in part, "Now, therefore, I, George Bush, President of the United States of America, do hereby proclaim the decade beginning January 1, 1990, as the Decade of the Brain. I call upon all public officials and the people of the United States to observe that decade with appropriate programs, ceremonies, and activities."

February 14, 1859: Ferris Wheel Day
Birthday of George Washington Gale Ferris, inventor of the Ferris wheel. G.W.G. Ferris, an American engineer and inventor, is best remembered for inventing the Ferris wheel for the World's Columbian Exposition at Chicago in 1893. That Ferris wheel was 250 feet in diameter and had 36 coaches, each of which could carry 40 passengers.

March 19-22, 1998: Schmeckfest in Freeman, South Dakota
A German food festival. Bratwurst and sauerkraut, kuchen and pluma moos—just a few of the dishes served at this German "festival of tasting" held in beautiful South Dakota. Crowds average 8,000 each year.

April 4-10, 1998: National Reading a Road Map Week
To promote map reading as an enjoyable pastime and as a survival skill for all present, future, and backseat drivers. Motto: "Happiness is knowing how to read a road map."

May 22, 1967: *Mister Rogers' Neighborhood* premiers on television
Presbyterian minister Fred Rogers hosted the long-running PBS show that

featured humans interacting with puppets in make-believe land. Rogers provided the voices for many of the puppets. Our favorite? Cranky King Friday.

June 4-6, 1998: World Pork Expo
In praise of pigs and pork. Held at Iowa State Fairgrounds, this is the world's largest pork-specific event. No joke. It features free pork samples, musical entertainment, hog shows, hog sales, seminars, and a 250-foot long grill with simmering pork. The nation's best barbecues come to compete in the Great Pork BarbeQlossal. Draws over 60,000 people each year.

July 1-31 (annually): Anti-Boredom Month
Begun in 1985 to prevent boredom. This self-awareness event encourages people to examine whether they or people they know are experiencing "an extended period of boredom" in their lives. According to the Boring Institute, this can be a warning sign of deeper problems. Advice is offered on how to avoid and overcome boredom.

August 9 (annually): National Hand Holding Day
A day to take the opportunity to hold the hand of someone you hold dear.

September 1 (annually): Emma M. Nutt Day
Honoring the first female telephone operator, Emma M. Nutt, who reportedly began her professional career at Boston, Minnesota, in 1878. She worked as a telephone operator for 33 years.

October 1-31 (annually): National Toilet Tank Repair Month
Month-long observance dedicated to the value and benefits of a properly tuned toilet with special emphasis on do-it-yourself repairs and water conservation.

November 3, 1718: Sandwich Day
Birthday of John Montague, Four Earl of Sandwich, England's first lord of the admiralty, secretary of state for the northern department, postmaster general, and the man after whom the explorer Captain Cook named the Sandwich Islands in 1778. A rake and a gambler, he is said to have invented the sandwich as a timesaving meal while engaged in a 24-hour-long gambling session in 1762.

December 1-31 (annually): Bingo Month
In honor of the popular game. Bingo was created in 1929 by Edwin S. Lowe. This celebration honors its innovation and manufacture. Today Bingo has grown into a five-billion-a-year charitable fund-raiser.

PAUSE

Segue from those silly dates to the Bible-study part of the lesson with words something like this:

There are all kinds of questions in the world, and there are plenty of people who think they have the answers. Some of these people, though, do the

same thing you just did in the game—they make up answers that sound good on the surface but in fact are far from the truth, especially when it comes to the really big questions that deal with God, fate, evil, death, and the meaning of life.

Christians are supposed to go the Bible and God for the answers. But what if the answers aren't clear even then? Is it okay to express our doubts, complaints, confusion, and disbelief to God? Habakkuk clears up some of the confusion for us—not about the big questions, but about our relationship and dialogue with God.

PONDER POINT - *option 1*
HABAKKUK'S COMPLAINT

Divide students into two groups. Have the first group read Habakkuk 1:1-4, and then rephrase Habakkuk's *complaint/question* in today's language for today's world.

Have the second group read Habakkuk 1:5-11 and rephrase *God's answer* for today's world. Give them just a few minutes to do this, and then gather as a large group. Ask one person from each group give their rephrased complaint/question aloud. Then discuss the following questions:

- **Where do many non-Christians (and perhaps some Christians) look for answers to some of life's deep questions? Talk about what these sources say and teach.**
- **How do you think God feels when we ask him life's deep questions? Explain.**
- **Talk about some of the social/global/environmental/other issues that Christians might question God about. How do you think most Christians want God to respond to these issues?**
- **How do you feel about God's answer to Habakkuk, "I am going to use something wicked and evil to accomplish my purposes"?**
- **Do you think God still uses wicked and evil things/people to accomplish his purposes today? Explain.**
- **Do you think there's a difference between God using something wicked and evil to accomplish his purpose and God causing something wicked and evil to happen? Discuss this.**
- **Why doesn't God just snap his fingers and fix the suffering, pain, and evil in the world? Explain.**

PONDER POINT - *option 2*
HABAKKUK'S RESPONSE

After God answered Habakkuk's question, what did Habakkuk do? Have someone read 2:1 to the group. Then divide your students into small groups of four or five. Give each group a copy of **Stop, Look, Listen** (page 66). After the groups have spent a few minutes working on the sheet, have them discuss the following question in their small group:

God, who controls the entire universe, is always ready and willing to stop and listen to each individual human being. We, who manage only our own lives, are not always ready and willing to stop and listen to God, the creator of the world. Why?

PONDER POINT - *option 3*
THOUGH AND YET

After stopping, looking, and listening to God, Habakkuk wrote a beautiful poem about the Lord. Read 3:17-19 to your students, emphasizing the words *though* and *yet*.

Hand out a copy of **Though and Yet** to each student (page 67). After several minutes, gather your students together and discuss the following questions:

- *How can we can keep our "thoughs" from controlling our thoughts and feelings?*
- *How can we can focus more clearly on our "yets"?*
- *For Christians, do you think the "yets" always beat out and are stronger than the "thoughs"? Explain.*

PAUSE

Segue into the next section, Personal Prescription, by saying something like this:

While not answering all our deep questions about God and life, Habakkuk reassures us that God is always there, ready to listen to us in our doubt and distress. He reminds us that the best way to discover God's answers is to stop, look, and listen. And he reassures us that the "yets" in our lives can take priority over the "thoughs"—if we are willing and determined.

PERSONAL PRESCRIPTION
HABAKKUK AND YOU

Give each student a copy of **Habakkuk and You** (page 68). Be sure they have Bibles. You might want to play quiet worship music during this time.

PRAYER

You can choose to let students silently pray the prayer at the end of the **Habakkuk and You** worksheet, or you can pray something like this yourself after a while:

God, thank you for the message of Habakkuk. Thank you that you're in control of the whole universe. Thank you that you also know each one of us intimately...and hear each of our prayers. This week, help us to take Habakkuk's words to heart so that we can become better listeners and followers of you. Amen.

Slips for the activity
Is That Your Final Answer?
in the Habakkuk session.
Photocopy this page, cut apart, and distribute at the appropriate point in the lesson.

January 1, 1990-December 31, 1999

February 14, 1859

March 19-22, 1998

April 4-10, 1998

May 22, 1967

June 4-6, 1998

July 1-31 (annually)

August 9, (annually)

September 1, (annually)

January 1-31 (annually)

November 3, 1718

December 1-31 (annually)

Think about ways that Christians today can **stop, look, and listen** for God. Then think about things that prevent Christians from stopping, looking, and listening for God. Write your thoughts below.

<u>Ways to</u>

Stop

Look

Listen

<u>Things that prevent</u>

Stopping

Looking

Listening

THOUGH & YET

Habakkuk 3:17 lists three "thoughs" that were very critical to survival in his day. Below, make a list of "thoughs" in your life. They can include disappointments, questions, circumstances, or anything else that might make you doubt God's love and care for you.

My personal "though" woes:

In the very next verse, Habakkuk finishes his thought. After all his "thoughs" are out in the open, he adds a "yet." Read through your list of "though woes," and then write a personal "yet" that declares your hope in God and love for him despite your "though woes."

My personal "yet":

Habakkuk and You
(personal prescription)

God, why...?

If you were face to face with God and could ask him to answer or explain one thing, what would it be? Write it below.

The following psalms aren't answers as much as they are assurances of God's presence and deep love for you. Take some time and read through them.

- Psalm 8
- Psalm 16
- Psalm 19
- Psalm 24
- Psalm 27
- Psalm 29
- Psalm 33

What do you think God wants to say to you about his love, his care, and his interest in every detail of your life?

You may want to silently pray a prayer like this:

God, I don't always understand you. I don't always understand life. I know that you've heard my question. Give me the patience I need to stop, look, and listen while I wait for your response. Please help me learn how to focus on the "yets" during the "thoughs" in my life. Amen.

DANIEL
A Man of Integrity, Wisdom, and Courage

PUNDITS

Daniel's confidence was not in prayer. His confidence rested in the God who answers prayer.
Following God, 158

A person of integrity [i.e., Daniel] is a powerful instrument in the hand of God.
Living Insights Study Bible, 872

Century after century, Daniel has shot adrenaline into the veins of God-obedience and put backbone into God-trust.
The Message, introduction to Old Testament prophets, 406

The book is thus written to encourage God's people to remain loyal and to assure them of God's power to keep them through their ordeal and of the certainty of the final victory of God's kingdom.
Prophets and Poets, 161

The theology of these stories [in Daniel] is "crisis theology." The issues are people of God are in a life-and-death situation. The issues are unmistakable...For us there appears to be no crisis. The edges are blurred. It is not easy to know how to act in our moral dilemmas. Indifference is sometimes a deadlier weapon against faith than the sword.
Prophets and Poets, 165

PROFILE

- Name means "God is (my) judge"
- Quoted by Jesus in Matthew 24:15
- Main character in some of best-known Bible stories
- Exiled from Judah to Babylon (site of present day Iraq) as a young teen in 605 B.C.
- Grew up during reign of King Josiah (one of the few good kings)
- Only prophet to receive apocalyptic prophecies in the form of dreams
- Chronological order of chapters—1, 2, 3, 4, 7, 8, 5, 9, 6, 10, 11, 12
- Contemporary of Ezekiel (which means that the Daniel in Ezekiel 14 is a different man)
- Became a powerful and trusted ruler in Babylon, serving under many different kings
- Was not a Detroit Lions fan

PURPOSE OF PROPHETIC PRONOUNCEMENTS
TO PROCLAIM GOD'S SOVEREIGNTY.

- God is the only God.
- God deserves our faithfulness in any and all circumstances.
- No one can serve two masters.

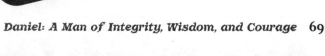

FROM OLD TO NEW
(where verses from this book are quoted in the New Testament)
Daniel 7:3-7 ↔ Revelation 13:1-2
Daniel 7:10 ↔ Revelation 20:12
Daniel 7:13-14 ↔ Matthew 24:30, Mark 13:26, Luke 21:27
Daniel 9:27 ↔ Matthew 24:15, Mark 13:14
(check out the Book of Revelation for additional Daniel references)

Daniel, a young Jew exiled to Babylon, was one of a group of young men chosen to enter training for the king's court. The young men were all of noble blood, handsome, intelligent, well informed, and "qualified to serve in the king's palace" (1:4). They were taught both the language and literature of Babylon. Perhaps the Babylonian king hoped to convert these young men into loyal subjects, thereby preventing the possibility of rebellion.

The first six chapters relay five narrative stories about Daniel's life:

Story 1. Daniel and his friends insist on following their own dietary regimen while in training, and they end up being the healthiest of all.

Story 2. King Nebuchadnezzar (let's just call him Neb) has a dream that he can't remember. None of his wise men can recall the dream for him, so of course neither can they interpret it. Daniel prays for wisdom and is able to do both. He becomes one of Neb's favorites.

Story 3. Daniel's three friends Shadrach, Meshach, and Abednego refuse to worship Neb's image of gold. They're thrown into the fiery furnace where a fourth man joins them. They survive the flames and become three of Neb's favorites.

Story 4. Neb's heir, King Belshazzar, a wicked man, sees a floating hand write on the wall of the palace during one of his extended revelries. Daniel is summoned to translate the writing, which extends judgment on Bel for rejecting God. Daniel becomes one of Bel's favorites. Too little, too late...Bel dies that night.

Story 5. The new king of Babylon, Darius, quickly recognizes Daniel as a wise and good man. Not as smart as Daniel, Darius gets tricked by some of his underlings (who hate Daniel) into enacting a new law that prohibits his subjects from praying to anyone but him for the next 30 days. Daniel obeys God ("thou shalt have no other gods before me") instead of the king, and as a result finds himself locked in a den of lions. Miraculously, the lions don't touch Daniel, and Daniel becomes a super-favorite of Darius.

After the five stories are six chapters of apocalyptic visions concerning Israel's future and the world's future. Based on those chapters, many soothsayers have predicted when the world will end. So far, they've all been wrong.

PRECEPTS & PRINCIPLES
PRICELESS POETRY AND PROSE FROM DANIEL

Then Daniel praised the God of heaven and said: "Praise be to the name of God for ever and ever; wisdom and power are his. He changes times and seasons; he sets up kings and deposes them. He gives wisdom to the wise and knowledge to the discerning. He reveals deep and hidden things; he knows what lies in darkness, and light dwells with him. I thank and praise you, O God of my fathers..." (Daniel 2:19b-23a)

Daniel replied, "No wise man, enchanter, magician or diviner can explain to the king the mystery he has asked about, but there is a God in heaven who reveals mysteries" (2:27, 28b).

Then Nebuchadnezzar said, "Praise be to the God of Shadrach, Meshach and Abednego, who has sent his angel and rescued his servants! They trusted in him and defied the king's command and were willing to give up their lives rather than serve or worship any god except their own God" (3:28).

His dominion is an eternal dominion; his kingdom endures from generation to generation. All the peoples of the earth are regarded as nothing. He does as he pleases with the powers of heaven and the peoples of the earth. No one can hold back his hand or say to him: "What have you done?" (4:34b-35).

Give ear, O God, and hear; open your eyes and see the desolation of the city that bears your Name. We do not make requests of you because we are righteous but because of your great mercy. (9:18)

PLAY - option 1

This is a *spontaneous melodrama*—one of those boisterous, no-rehearsal, slapsticky skits that get kids involved, whether they're hamming up front as impromptu actors, or in the audience cheering for the good guys, hissing the bad guys, and getting nearly as animated as the onstage actors. It's also an effective (albeit goofy) introduction to a biblical point.

Here's how to get the most mileage out of this spontaneous melodrama:

Get your actors up front, assign them their parts (animate or inanimate), and tell them to do—in a broad, hammy way—whatever you read. When you read something like, "And the frog croaked, 'Okay, have it your way'—and promptly fell over dead," the croakier the student frog's voice as he repeats the line and the more outlandish his falling over and twitching in his death throes, the better.

Before the meeting, read through **Daniel in His TV Den** (page 74) so you have a feel for the script. Then at the meeting when it's time for the skit, recruit 10 students up to center stage as the cast of this spontaneous melodrama.

With your actors up front with you, tell them that you'll narrate the spontaneous melodrama—and that when in the story you describe something that one of the students' characters is doing, they act it out. If you read that a character says something, the appropriate student says it. If you read that a character does something, the appropriate student does it. The kids' acting and speaking should be outlandish and big and bold.

Okay...on with the show!

PLAY - option 2

From the video *Wild America*, play the clip in which the three brothers are in the Cave of Bears. In Daniel's case, the lions probably started out wild and were then subdued by angels. In this case, the bears started out asleep and then woke up wild and furious. Great scene! (1:09:45—1:16:15)

PAUSE

Segue from this fun stuff to the Bible-study part of the lesson by saying something like this:

It's easy to miss the point of stories if we've heard them over and over and over again. The Book of Daniel contains some of the best-known Bible stories ever written. Most kids learn them in Sunday school. But the Daniel

stories are more than well known. They're also timeless. They have as much to say to us today as they did to the people who first heard them. They have new things to say to us each time we read them. And they have new things to say to us in each of our life stages. Daniel's stories, especially, offer teens some great looks at integrity, wisdom, and courage—things that aren't focused on too much today.

PONDER POINT

In order to cover as many parts of Daniel's story as possible, the Ponder Points for this lesson will be addressed simultaneously by several groups, and they will eventually share insights and ideas with the entire group.

Divide into groups of four or five. Give each group one of the **Book Review** versions (pages 75-78); since there are only four different **Book Reviews**, it's okay if more than one group gets the same version. Here are the four different worksheets:

- **Daniel in Training (chapter 1)**
- **Daniel and the Dream (chapter 2:1-28, 46-49)**
- **Daniel and the Writing Hand (chapter 5:1-17, 29-30)**
- **Daniel in the Lions' Den (chapter 6)**

Each book review asks students to offer examples of integrity, wisdom, and courage.

Give your students at least 10 to 15 minutes to work on this. Then call them together to share their answers and ideas with each other. First listen to all the integrity examples, then all the wisdom examples, and then the courage examples.

Then discuss the following questions:

- *Name some well-known people today known for their integrity, wisdom, and/or courage.*
- *In what ways does today's society encourage people to pursue or discourage people from pursuing integrity, wisdom, and/or courage? Which action—encourage or discourage—do you think is stronger? Explain.*
- *Most of us don't face the kind of crises Daniel did—the threat of being killed for following Christ. Talk about some of the hard situations you do face where you must decide how to act or what to say. How does your faith come into play? Have you shown integrity, courage, and wisdom? Have others noticed?*

Have different students read the following verses dealing with the pursuit of integrity, wisdom, and courage:

Integrity. Psalms 1:1-3, Romans 12:2, 2 Thessalonians 2:13-15
Wisdom. 2 Timothy 3:14-15, James 1:5, James 3:17
Strength/Courage. Psalm 28:7, Psalm 73:26, Isaiah 40:31

After each verse, ask the group what the Scriptures teach about the source and practice of integrity, wisdom, and courage.

PAUSE

Segue into the next section, Personal Prescription, with words to this effect:

Daniel is famous because of the amazing events in his life. Most of us will never face the threat of death simply for living out our faith. And almost assuredly, none of us will ever face that threat multiple times. But Daniel wasn't great only in the midst of those amazing events. His faith—practiced on a daily basis—enabled Daniel to stand up to the trials he faced. He never sought fame. He never talked proudly about himself. He simply lived an obedient life in everything, from his daily physical health to his daily pursuit of God.

PERSONAL PRESCRIPTION

Lead your students in thinking about the message of Daniel's life:
- **Worship God only.**
- **Be obedient even when it's dangerous.**
- **Trust God to take care of you.**
- **Do not think too highly of yourself.**

Hand out index cards to everyone, and say something like this:

Now think about yourself. What part of Daniel's message is speaking to you? What can you do to begin developing integrity, wisdom, and courage? Write a brief message to yourself below about those things. Think back to the verses we read about integrity, wisdom, and courage. Choose one or two to focus on this week, write them on the index card, and keep them in your pocket or hang them in your locker. Be sure to think and pray about this issue during the week.

PRAYER

Have students regather into the groups used for the Ponder Points. Tell them to take turns praying aloud (if they're comfortable doing that) about the things discussed during this lesson. If some want to, they can share what they wrote on their index card (in Personal Prescription, above). After a few minutes, close the lesson with a prayer like this—

Dear God,
Being young men and women of integrity is difficult. Every day we face the temptation to live for ourselves, to compromise our beliefs, or to do less than our best. Begin working in our hearts, giving us the strength and wisdom to live obediently every single day, as Daniel did. Amen.

Daniel in His TV Den
A spontaneous melodrama

CAST:
Daniel
Chair
Table (2 students)
Angel
Cats (3 of 'em)
TV actors (2)

PROPS:
Bathrobe (for Daniel)
Ear headbands or eyeliner whiskers
(for Cats)
Clean white T-shirt (for angel)

All actors start the spontaneous melodrama offstage—in the hall outside the youth room door, etc.—and enter when cued by the narrator's lines.

Once upon a time, a really good guy named Daniel returned home after buying a new TV. He carried the TV into his den where his favorite chair and coffee table were, plugged it in, and then sat down to begin channel surfing. First he watched some actors do a cooking show on how to make gourmet PB and J sandwiches. Then he channel surfed to a professional wrestling match where one wrestler was ready to body slam the other. Then he switched to a daytime talk show featuring "People who've had the hiccups for more than a month." Then he switched to a concert featuring some opera solos. Finally Dan exclaimed, "I hate TV!" Then he got up and kicked the TV so hard that the opera singers faded away and the screen went blank. Just then, an angel entered and said—in a very angelic voice—"Hey Dan! Watch out! There are three nasty alley cats heading straight for your den!" Then the angel screamed "LOOK OUT!" three times at the top of his or her lungs. Suddenly, three huge cats leaped into Daniel's den while making constant cat noises. The angel fainted while making angel-fainting sounds. The first cat ran to the fainted angel, stood on top of it, and started hissing in its face. The second cat ran to Daniel and came right up to him, ready to attack. The third cat crawled under the table and started cleaning her paws by licking them. Just then, the angel woke up and yelled, "Never fear! Angel is here!" He or she put the first cat in a chokehold and said, "This is Dan's den, you dastardly dimwit!" Dan threw the second cat over his shoulders, spun the cat around six times, and threw the cat to the floor where the cat twitched for a few seconds and then lay lifeless. The angel continued keeping the first cat in a chokehold. The third cat crawled out from under the table, jumped onto the chair, and curled up to take a nap. The first cat finally gave up fighting with the angel, the angel released him, and the cat curled up and begin meowing like a frightened—err, umm—kitten. The angel high-fived Dan and said, "Dan! You da man!" The angel left, fluttering its wings frantically and singing, "I can fly! I can fly! I can fly!" The three cats ran away, yowling and hissing loudly. Dan sat back down on his chair, rested his feet on the table, and said, "All right, who stole the remote!?"

The End

Book Review
Daniel in Training

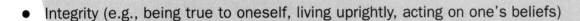

Daniel 1

First, read Daniel chapter 1 about Daniel in training —either individually or as a group.

Now, within the chapter, identify examples of how Daniel fulfills the three bulleted virtues listed below. Describe the examples and jot down the verse(s) where you find your examples. Need a creative nudge? Check out Jump starters at the bottom of the page.

- Integrity (e.g., being true to oneself, living uprightly, acting on one's beliefs)

- Wisdom (e.g., thinking before acting or speaking, taking time to examine a situation before reacting)

- Courage

Jump starters
- Imagine being moved to a strange school, against your will, during your freshman or sophomore year.
- Imagine that you and your friends are offered high-paying jobs at a nearby sporting goods store, and you say no because you just made a yearlong commitment at your present job.
- Notice that Daniel resolved not to defile himself.
- Imagine being captain of a winning varsity team, valedictorian of your class, president of the student body, voted "Most Popular" in your school, but not having any ego.

Book Review
Daniel and the Dream

Daniel
2:1-28,
46-49

First, read the verses in Daniel chapter 2 listed above about Daniel and the dream—either individually or as a group.

Now, within the chapter, identify examples of how Daniel fulfills the three bulleted virtues listed below. Describe the examples and jot down the verse(s) where you find your examples. Need a creative nudge? Check out Jump starters at the bottom of the page.

• Integrity (e.g., being true to oneself, living uprightly, acting on one's beliefs)

• Wisdom (e.g., thinking before acting or speaking, taking time to examine a situation before reacting)

• Courage

Jump starters
• Imagine volunteering to solve a problem that many others who are more experienced than you have already failed at.
• Imagine if the price of failing to solve the problem was death.
• Notice that Daniel speaks with wisdom and tact, and that he takes time to gather information and pray before making any commitments or speaking.
• Imagine that a king bows before you and offers you anything you want.

Book Review
Daniel and the writing hand

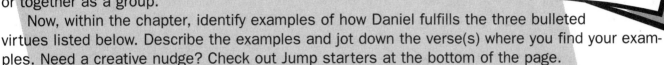

Daniel 5:1-17, 29-30

First, read the verses in Daniel chapter 5 listed above about Daniel and the writing hand—either individually or together as a group.

Now, within the chapter, identify examples of how Daniel fulfills the three bulleted virtues listed below. Describe the examples and jot down the verse(s) where you find your examples. Need a creative nudge? Check out Jump starters at the bottom of the page.

● Integrity (e.g., being true to oneself, living uprightly, acting on one's beliefs)

● Wisdom (e.g., thinking before acting or speaking, taking time to examine a situation before reacting)

● Courage

Jump starters
- Imagine being ignored for 23 years.
- Imagine being offered power and riches just for doing what you do best.
- Imagine having to personally deliver news of someone's impending death.
- Imagine if that person had the power to kill you.
- Notice that Daniel would not let Belshazzar buy him with promises of power and wealth.

Book Review
Daniel in the Lions' Den

Daniel
6

First, read Daniel chapter 6 about Daniel in the
den of lions—either individually or together as a group.
    Now, within the chapter, identify examples of how Daniel fulfills the three bulleted
virtues listed below. Describe the examples and jot down the verse(s) where you find your examples.
Need a creative nudge? Check out Jump starters at the bottom of the page.

● Integrity (e.g., being true to oneself, living uprightly, acting on one's beliefs)

● Wisdom (e.g., thinking before acting or speaking, taking time to examine a situation before reacting)

● Courage

Jump starters
● **Notice that Daniel, an honest and good
  man, had many enemies.**
● **Imagine being told that praying to God
  put you on death row.**
● **Image walking to your death...willingly.**

JEREMIAH
(part 1)
The Man

PUNDITS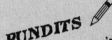

[Jeremiah] reminds us, in an era of artificial cheer and television smiles, that God's message is not always comforting and encouraging.
NIV Student Bible,
introduction to Jeremiah, 660

Jeremiah's was a soul in pain, stern with gloom.
Prophets, 105

The tragic figure of Jeremiah is in many ways similar to Christ, who even more was despised and rejected by men. His book is a valuable reminder that God does not ask us to be successful, but to be faithful.
The Sacred Sixty-Six, 165

By any human measurement, Jeremiah was probably the outstanding failure in the Bible. For 49 years he proclaimed God's will to the people, but apparently no one listened to him.
The Sacred Sixty-Six, 162

Jeremiah did not think that evil was inevitable. Over and above man's blindness stood the wonder of repentance, the open gateway through which man could enter if he would.
The Prophets, 104

[Jeremiah] was a person overwhelmed by sympathy for God and sympathy for man. Standing before the people he pleaded for God; standing before God he pleaded for his people.
The Prophets, 121

In looking for a companion who has lived through catastrophic disruption and survived with grace, biblical people more often than not come upon Jeremiah and receive him as a true, honest, and God-revealing companion for the worst of times.
The Message,
introduction to Jeremiah, 157

PROFILE
- Name means "the Lord throws"

- Revealed his emotions and personal life more than any other prophet

- Prophesied from 626-586 B.C.

- Contemporary of Habakkuk

- Contemporary of Ezekiel (who prophesied to the exiles in Babylon)

FROM OLD TO NEW
(where verses from this book are quoted in the New Testament)

Jeremiah 7:11	↔ Matthew 21:13, Mark 11:17, Luke 19:46
Jeremiah 9:24	↔ 1 Corinthians 1:31, 2 Corinthians 10:17

However we approach Jeremiah, one thing is clear: that discipleship is costly.
Prophets and Poets, 94

PURPOSE OF PROPHETIC PRONOUNCEMENTS
TO WARN GOD'S PEOPLE THAT JUDGMENT AWAITS THOSE WHO INSIST ON DOING EVIL.

- Discipleship is costly.
- God will honor sincere repentance.
- Individuals are personally responsible for their behavior.

PREVIEW
A PEEK AT THE PITH OF JEREMIAH

Jeremiah ministered for more than 40 turbulent years in Judah's history. Israel had fallen to the Assyrians almost 100 years earlier and no longer existed as a nation. Though his messages are directed to Judah, they are sometimes referred to as "Israel." Because his book is not in chronological order, it's nearly impossible to dissect and understand without some references or commentaries close at hand.

One way to sift through the confusion is by paying attention to which king was reigning when he delivered specific prophecies. The five kings who sat on the throne during Jeremiah's ministry were—

- Josiah (640-609). A God-fearing king who restored proper temple worship, destroyed idols, and taught his people the Law of Moses. He was killed in battle by the king of Egypt.
- Jehoahaz (609-609). Son of Josiah, chosen by countrymen to replace his father. After reigning only three months, the king of Egypt took him captive, dethroned him, and replaced him with...
- Jehoiakim (609-598). An evil king during whose reign (in 605 B.C., to be exact) Babylon invaded Judah and took hostages into exile, including Daniel.
- Jehoiachin (598-597). Became king at age 18 and reigned for three months. Babylon invaded Judah again, this time attacking the capital city, Jerusalem. The king, his wives, his officials, and thousands of others were exiled to Babylon.
- Zedekiah (597-587). Uncle of Jehoiachin. Evil dude. Decided he was tired of being controlled by a Babylonian king. So Babylon attacked Jerusalem again, this time destroying the city walls, burning the palace and temple, and exiling most of the remaining citizens. Jeremiah stayed behind with a few of the "poorest people of the land" (2 Kings 25:12).

As you can see, Jeremiah prophesied during dark and turbulent years. He was aware of how grim the situation was, and it shows in his writing. Shortly after Jerusalem was destroyed in 587/586 B.C., Jeremiah was dragged off to Egypt by his fellow non-exiled countrymen, where tradition says he was eventually stoned to death.

JEREMIAH 101
For those not familiar with Jeremiah's story, you can get a chronological overview of the action by reading the following chapters and verses in the order listed: 1, 26, 11:18-23, 18, 20, 36, 21, 27-29, 34:1-7, 37:1-10, 34:8-22, 37:11-38:13, 32, 38:14-39:14, 52, 40-44.

Before I formed you in the womb I knew you, before you were born I set you apart; I appointed you as a prophet to the nations. (Jeremiah 1:5)

This is what the Lord says: "Let not the wise man boast of his wisdom or the strong man boast of his strength or the rich man boast of his riches, but let him who boasts boast about this: that he understands and knows me, that I am the Lord, who exercises kindness, justice and righteousness on earth, for in these I delight," declares the Lord. (9:23-24)

Blessed is the man who trusts in the Lord, whose confidence is in him. He will be like a tree planted by the water that sends out its roots by the stream. (17:7-8)

So the word of the Lord has brought me insult and reproach all day long. But if I say, "I will not mention him or speak any more in his name," his word is in my heart like a fire, a fire shut up in my bones. I am weary of holding it in; indeed, I cannot. (20:8-9)

You will seek me and find me when you seek me with all your heart. (29:13)

This is what the Lord says, he who made the earth, the Lord who formed it and established it—the Lord is his name: "Call to me and I will answer you and tell you great and unsearchable things you do not know" (33:2-3).

PLAY

Jeremiah is often called "the prophet of doom" because of his harsh statements. Case in point:

Circumcise yourselves to the Lord, circumcise your hearts, you men of Judah and people of Jerusalem, or my wrath will break out and burn like fire because of the evil you have done—burn with no one to quench it. (4:4)

Cartoonists and commentators have made good use of prophet humor based on the image of a doomsday prophet.

Divide your students into small groups (you'll need poster board and markers). Assign each group one of the following identities as numbers allow:

- **Computer geek**
- **Pro football player**
- **Teacher**
- **Parent**
- **Astronaut**
- **Pro hockey player**
- **Rodeo star**
- **NASCAR racer**
- **Fashion model**
- **Dentist**
- **Pro wrestler**

...et cetera. Now tell students to create a Doomsday Sign that reflects the identity of their specific group. For example:

Hockey player: *The end is near—my last tooth just got knocked out!*
Astronaut: *The end is near—they're sending me to Pluto!*

When the groups are done, have a student from each group read its sign and let the other groups guess the identity of the "prophet."

PAUSE

Segue from the doomsday game to the Bible-study part of the lesson with words to this effect:

Many people envision a prophet as a crazy old guy with a long beard, wearing a robe, standing on street corners, carrying a woe is me sign, and yelling, "The end is near! The sky is falling! Doomsday is just around the corner!"

At first glance, Jeremiah may seem like that. He was moody, determined, and very in-your-face. But underneath all of that was a tortured soul whose moodiness and sorrow and determination were a reflection of God's own heart and experience.

PONDER POINT - option 1
OUR INADEQUACY

Show the clip from the movie *Simon Birch* where he stands up in his church pew on Sunday morning and says, "What do donuts and coffee have to do with worship?" (27:59—32:39)

Simon had several things going against him—his age, his size, and his unpopular message. He was plainly inadequate as a person (so nearly everyone thought), particularly as a person with a supposed mission from God.

Like Simon, Jeremiah felt he was inadequate as a prophet. Have a few students read Jeremiah 1:4-10 and 1:17-19 aloud. Discuss the following questions:

- **Why might Jeremiah have thought his young age made him inadequate to do God's work?**
- **Have you ever felt that your age makes you inadequate to do certain things? Describe those situations.**
- **Do you think adults consider teens to be inadequate for certain roles or jobs in a family? In society? In church? Talk about these things.**
- **In terms of serving God, what are advantages/disadvantages of being a teenager? Explain.**
- **In terms of serving God, what are advantages/disadvantages of being inadequate? Explain.**
- **How would you feel if God clearly told you what he wanted you to do with the rest of your life? Consider both the positive and negative sides of such a revelation, and discuss them.**

On a marker board make two columns, one titled AGE and the other ABILITY. Ask your students to think of Bible characters other than Jeremiah who served God in spite of their inadequate ages or abilities. (e.g., Joseph was young…King David was young…Mary was young…Paul was a poor public speaker…Moses was afraid of public speaking.)

Have two volunteers read the following passages aloud to the group:
- 1 Kings 3:7-9 (young King Solomon asking for wisdom)
- 1 Timothy 4:12 (encouragement to young Timothy to be a role model to others)

PONDER POINT - *option 2*
A PROPHET'S DESPAIR

In Jeremiah 20:7-9, 14, 18, the prophet describes how God has ruined his life. Read it to your students. The translation *The Message* captures Jeremiah's emotions particularly well:

You pushed me into this, God, and I let you do it. You were too much for me. And now I'm a public joke. They all poke fun at me. Every time I open my mouth I'm shouting, "Murder!" or "Rape!" And all I get for my god-warnings are insults and contempt. But if I say, "Forget it! No more God-Messages from me!" the words are fire in my belly, a burning in my bones. I'm worn out trying to hold it in. I can't do it any longer!…Curse the day I was born! The day my mother bore me—a curse on it, I say!…Why, oh why, did I ever leave that womb? Life's been nothing but trouble and tears, and what's coming is more of the same.

Imagine feeling this way for an entire lifetime. The cost of Jeremiah's mission was high:

- **He was prohibited from marrying (16:1-4).**
- **People plotted against his life (11:18-23, 18:18-23).**
- **He was whipped and locked up (20:1-2).**
- **He was rejected by friends (20:10).**
- **He was nearly killed by a mob (26:7-16).**
- **He was falsely accused and imprisoned (37:11-16).**
- **He was left to die in a mud pit (38:1-6).**
- **He was taken hostage by his countrymen (43:1-7).**

Through all of this, Jeremiah was still able to say—

Lord, you are my strength and fortress, my refuge in the day of trouble!… O Lord, you alone can heal me; you alone can save. My praises are for you alone!… Your words are what sustain me. They bring me great joy and are my heart's delight, for I bear your name, O Lord God Almighty…. Lord, there is no one like you! For you are great, and your name is full of power. (16:19, 17:14, 15:16, 10:6, NLT)

It's fair to say that God did indeed "ruin" Jeremiah's life—but what a wonderful thing it was!

Give each student a copy of **Radically Ruined** (page 87). Students can work alone or in small groups. The discussion questions at the end of the handout can be explored in small groups, or all together. Here are those questions:

- **Talk about ways that God has "ruined" your life.**

- **Following Christ involves a cost, but it also offers benefits. Talk about some benefits you personally experience because of following Christ. Are there other benefits that you'd like to experience but haven't? Talk about these and discuss when and how you might experience them.**

- **How do you personally deal with the hardships of following Christ (rejection, ridicule, temptation, self-denial, et cetera)? Share some examples.**

PONDER POINT - option 3
THE TURMOIL OF GOD

Jeremiah's deep emotions may have been a result of his turbulent experiences as a prophet. Or perhaps God chose him to be a prophet precisely because he was a deeply emotional man. Jeremiah may have proclaimed God's wrath to the people, but he *lived* God's wrath inwardly. The turmoil he experienced as a result of both loving and despising the people was a reflection of the same turmoil God experienced.

The ultimate purpose of a prophet is not to be inspired, but to inspire the people; not to be filled with a passion, but to impassion the people with understanding for God. (The Prophets, 115)

The following passages in the book of Jeremiah communicate some of his feelings:

- 4:19-21
- 6:10-11
- 8:18-9:2
- 10:19-21
- 13:15-17
- 23:9-10

The following passages communicate some of God's feelings—

- 2:26-32
- 4:14
- 6:1-2
- 14:17-18
- 18:11-13
- 32:30-35
- 32:36-42

There are several ways you can introduce your students to the turmoil of both Jeremiah and God. Choose from the following—

Reflect

In small groups, have students read some of the passages listed above. You can have each group do a combination from the two lists (Jeremiah's feelings and God's feelings), or you can have half the groups read about Jeremiah and half read about God. For each passage they should talk about—

- **The *kinds* of emotions and the *cause* of the emotions.**
- **Times when they've experienced similar emotions.**
- **Parallel circumstances in today's world (e.g., things the church might do to anger/grieve God).**

Record

Have students choose one passage from each list (Jeremiah's feelings and God's feelings). Then have them write about similar experiences in their own lives (things they've experienced personally that caused *them* to feel deep emotions, and things they did personally that probably caused *God* to feel deep emotions).

Rewrite

In groups or all together, choose one passage from each list (Jeremiah's feelings and God's feelings). Have students work together to rewrite it for current situations in society and/or the church. For example, Jeremiah 6:10-11 could be rewritten this way—

It doesn't matter what I say. No one listens. And no one cares. Whenever they try to teach me that people started out as a fish or an ape or a strange little blob of nothingness, I want to tell them they're wrong. I started out as a well-planned set of blueprints drawn by God himself—everyone started out that way. But they think I'm stupid, a Jesus freak who doesn't know anything. It makes me so mad! Not because I care whether or not they listen to me...but because I want them to know the truth.

Have some students read their rewrites to the group.

PAUSE

Segue into the next section, Personal Prescription, by saying something like this:

Jeremiah's book has a lot to say to us today. Like Jeremiah, we live in turbulent times. Globally, there is upheaval among nations. In our own nation, people struggle with pride, injustice, and greed. In the church, there's always the danger of saying one thing but doing another. Christians face a daily challenge of staying faithful to God when politics, economics, and society are topsy-turvy. Jeremiah lived through all those things—starting at a young age—and he did it by relying on God.

PERSONAL PRESCRIPTION
JEREMIAH AND YOU

Give each student a copy of **Jeremiah and You** (page 88), which focuses on Ponder Point/option 1. After giving students a few minutes to read the Personal Prescription, have them get into pairs or small groups and share their thoughts with each other. Encourage them to pray for each other during the week.

LIVING DANGEROUSLY
Can you say this about yourself?

"I'm ready for a Christianity that 'ruins' my life (a holy disruption where Jesus turns my life upside-down in order to make it right-side up), that captures my heart and makes me uncomfortable. I want to be filled with an astonishment which is so captivating that I am considered wild and unpredictable and...well...dangerous" (Michael Yaconelli, "Dangerous Wonder," 24).

If not, then maybe you need to take some time to reacquaint yourself with guys like Jeremiah. And Jesus. Living for God means living dangerously. Who'd want it any other way?

RADICALLY RUINED

Mark 8:34-37

Luke 14:25-33

John 12:23-26

Ephesians 6:11-12

Romans 12:1-2

Are you, like Jeremiah, willing to pay the price of following God full on, 100 percent ? And when it feels like your life has been ruined, will you be able to say, "I wouldn't have it any other way" ?

◎ Talk about ways that God has "ruined" your life.

◎ Following Christ involves a cost, but it also offers benefits. Talk about some of the benefits you personally experience because of following Christ. Are there other benefits that you'd like to experience but haven't ? Talk about these and discuss when and how you might experience them.

◎ How do you personally deal with the hardships of following Christ (rejection, ridicule, temptation, self-denial, et cetera) ? Share some examples.

Jeremiah and You
(personal prescription)

"Hi. My name is Taylor, and I'm inadequate."
The first step in any recovery program is recognizing and admitting the truth. When a person becomes a Christian, the first step is recognizing and admitting sinfulness. When a Christian becomes a servant of God (and not all Christians are necessarily in that category), the first step is recognizing and admitting inadequacy.

Why? Because as long as we think we're good enough and capable enough to serve God on our own, we'll never get much done. All people are always inadequate, writes Eugene Peterson in *Run with the Horses*. Yet we often pretend that we're not...unless some task comes along that we're not very excited about. Then we're happy to admit our inadequacy:

- I'm not talented enough

- I'm not popular enough

- I'm only a high school student

- I'm not good at meeting new people

- I can't talk in front of a group

...blah blah blah...

Jeremiah admitted his inadequacy. "I can't speak for you," he protested to God. "I'm too young. I don't have any training." It's not that he was trying to avoid the work. He was just being honest, and God knew it. So what did God do? He didn't yell, condemn, or punish Jeremiah. Instead God encouraged him. "Come on, Jeremiah, don't say that. I know you're young and inexperienced, but it doesn't matter. I'll be with you. I'll give you the words. I'll make you adequate."

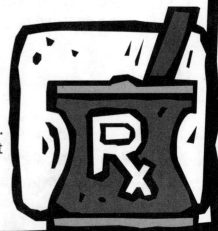

JEREMIAH
(part 2)
Persistence in Action

PUNDITS

The secret of [Jeremiah's] persevering pilgrimage—not thinking with dread about the long road ahead but greeting the present moment, greeting every present moment, with obedient delight, with expectant hope.

Run with the Horses, 114

The mark of a certain kind of genius is the ability and energy to keep returning to the same task relentlessly, imaginatively, curiously, for a lifetime.

Run with the Horses, 118

[Jeremiah 25:3-4] is the clue to our erratic life patterns, our inconstancy, our unfaithfulness, our stupid inability to distinguish between fashion and faith: we don't rise up early and listen to God. We don't daily find a time apart from the crowd, a time of silence and solitude, for preparing for the day's journey.

Run with the Horses, 118

Now, through the prophets, God turns instead to the power of the word. Evidently God does not consider "mere words" an inferior form of proof, for he chose the prophets to communicate the anguish God himself felt…one important message shines through with great force: God passionately desires his people.

The Bible Jesus Read, 176

PROFILE

- Wrote longest book, according to word count, in the Bible

- Forbidden by God to marry

- Sometimes referred to as the Weeping Prophet or the Prophet of Doom

- Wrote book of Lamentations as well as the prophetic book named after him

PURPOSE OF PROPHETIC PRONOUNCEMENTS

TO WARN GOD'S PEOPLE THAT JUDGMENT AWAITS THOSE WHO INSIST ON DOING EVIL.

- Discipleship is costly.
- God will honor sincere repentance.
- Individuals are personally responsible for their behavior.

FROM OLD TO NEW
(where verses from this book are quoted in the New Testament)

Jeremiah 31:15 → Matthew 2:18
Jeremiah 31:31-34 → Hebrews 8:8-12, 10:16-17
Jeremiah 32:38 → 2 Corinthians 6:16

Jeremiah ministered for more than 40 turbulent years in Judah's history. Israel had fallen to the Assyrians almost 100 years earlier and no longer existed as a nation. Though his messages are directed to Judah, they are sometimes referred to as "Israel." Because his book is not in chronological order, it's nearly impossible to dissect and understand without some references or commentaries close at hand.

One way to sift through the confusion is by paying attention to which king was reigning when he delivered specific prophecies. The five kings who sat on the throne during Jeremiah's ministry were—

- **Josiah (640-609).** A God-fearing king who restored proper temple worship, destroyed idols, and taught his people the Law of Moses. He was killed in battle by the king of Egypt.

- **Jehoahaz (609-609).** Son of Josiah, chosen by countrymen to replace his father. After reigning only three months, the king of Egypt took him captive, dethroned him, and replaced him with...

- **Jehoiakim (609-598).** An evil king during whose reign (in 605 B.C., to be exact) Babylon invaded Judah and took hostages into exile, including Daniel.

- **Jehoiachin (598-597).** Became king at age 18 and reigned for three months. Babylon invaded Judah again, this time attacking the capital city, Jerusalem. The king, his wives, his officials, and thousands of others were exiled to Babylon.

- **Zedekiah (597-587).** Uncle of Jehoichin. Evil dude. Decided he was tired of being controlled by a Babylonian king. So Babylon attacked Jerusalem again, this time destroying the city walls, burning the palace and temple, and exiling most of the remaining citizens. Jeremiah stayed behind with a few of the "poorest people of the land" (2 Kings 25:12).

As you can see, Jeremiah prophesied during dark and turbulent years. He was aware of how grim the situation was, and it shows in his writing. Shortly after Jerusalem was destroyed in 587/586 B.C., Jeremiah was dragged off to Egypt by his fellow non-exiled countrymen, where tradition says he was eventually stoned to death.

JEREMIAH 101
For those not familiar with Jeremiah's story, you can get a chronological overview of the action by reading the following chapters and verses in the order listed: 1, 26, 11:18-23, 18, 20, 36, 21, 27-29, 34:1-7, 37:1-10, 34:8-22, 37:11-38:13, 32, 38:14-39:14, 52, 40-44.

PRECEPTS & PRINCIPLES
PRICELESS POETRY AND PROSE FROM JEREMIAH

Before I formed you in the womb I knew you, before you were born I set you apart; I appointed you as a prophet to the nations. (Jeremiah 1:5)

This is what the Lord says: "Let not the wise man boast of his wisdom or the strong man boast of his strength or the rich man boast of his riches, but let him who boasts boast about this: that he understands and knows me, that I am the Lord, who exercises kindness, justice and righteousness on earth, for in these I delight," declares the Lord. (9:23-24)

Blessed is the man who trusts in the Lord, whose confidence is in him. He will be like a tree planted by the water that sends out its roots by the stream. (17:7-8)

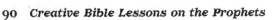

So the word of the Lord has brought me insult and reproach all day long. But if I say, "I will not mention him or speak any more in his name," his word is in my heart like a fire, a fire shut up in my bones. I am weary of holding it in; indeed, I cannot. (20:8-9)

You will seek me and find me when you seek me with all your heart. (29:13)

This is what the Lord says, he who made the earth, the Lord who formed it and established it—the Lord is his name: "Call to me and I will answer you and tell you great and unsearchable things you do not know" (33:2-3).

PLAY
STICKER WARS

Give each student five stickers (the cheap, colored, round, self-adhesive label kind). Explain that on your signal, the students' job is to put their stickers on other people (no stickers on hair, please)—as quickly (and gently) as possible. Stickees can remove them and stick them on someone else.

    The goal? To have the fewest stickers on when time's up—two or three minutes is plenty. Be sure to have music playing while they're stickering each other.

PAUSE

Segue from the sticker game to the Bible-study part of the lesson by saying something like:

Sometimes life feels like this game. You make a little progress, accomplish a few things, feel like you're winning finally—and then you're right back where you started: Stuck! It seems like you can't get ahead, like all you do is the same thing over and over and over again. That's what life was like for Jeremiah. For more than 40 years, he preached the same message to the same people, and for more than 40 years, he got the same response: Why don't you just leave us alone, prophet man?

PONDER POINT - *option 1*
THE PERSISTENT PROPHET

Show the clip in *Shawshank Redemption* at the end when Red (Morgan Freeman) describes the decades-long escape plan of Andy (Tim Robbins). (1:53:50—2:00:15)

    Talk to your students about patience, commitment, and willingness to keep working even when not seeing results. What kept Andy going? The knowledge that he was innocent and his hope for eventual freedom.

    Then pose this scenario: **Imagine if, after all that work, Andy couldn't break the pipe with the rock, that there were guard dogs waiting for him in the creek. The frustration and discouragement would have been overwhelming.**

    Which, in fact, accurately describes Jeremiah's life.

Have someone read Jeremiah 25:2, 3 to the group:

"So Jeremiah the prophet said to all the people of Judah and to all those living in Jerusalem: For twenty-three years—from the thirteenth year of Josiah son of Amon king of Judah until this very day—the word of the Lord has come to me and I have spoken to you again and again, but you have not listened."

That phrase again and again—it describes persistence. It comes from two Hebrew words that mean to do early in the morning...to do again and again and shoulder. (See the Zondervan NIV Exhaustive Concordance, Hebrew to English, entries 8899 and 8900.) Jeremiah is conveying this idea: "For 23 years I've gotten up early in the morning, day after day after day, and shouldered my responsibility of communicating God's Word to you stubborn people."

How did Jeremiah do it?

Do this exercise with your students:

1. On a marker board write the word PERSISTENCE.

2. Ask your students to suggest some other words that *persistence* reminds them of—like *dedication*, maybe, and *commitment*. List these words on one side of the board.

3. Then ask students to think of specific situations that require persistence, like attending and graduating from college. Have them list things that are needed in order to be persistent or dedicated in those particular situations. (Requirements for college, for example, include finishing daily homework, keeping the goal of graduation in sight, a desire to pursue a certain career, belief in one's ability, genuine interest in class topics and subjects, willingness to stick with the boring required courses, et cetera.)

4. Ask your students how persistent they think they'd be if they failed a basic required course not once, not twice—but many times.

5. When you've talked about this for a while, switch from the hypothetical situation to Jeremiah's situation, and ask this:

Based on what we've just discussed, on what you know about God, and on any personal experiences you've had of standing tough in the face of adversity, how do you think Jeremiah was able and willing to prophecy for so long to people who ignored him, hated him, laughed at him, punished him, told lies about him, and generally treated him like dirt?

After the students have discussed their own ideas about Jeremiah's persistence for a while, divide into small groups and distribute copies of **24/7** (page 97) for them to work on. This will give them a chance to see what scripture has to say about Jeremiah's persistence. When students have finished working on this worksheet, regather as a large group and ask for volunteers to share their answers. Be aware that the Bible passages that are referenced on **24/7** do not give explicit answers ("Jeremiah was persistent because he trusted God"). Instead students will have to read between the lines, will have to infer conclusions from what they read. Be ready to help them with this if needed. Some possible responses for **24/7**:

- 6:11 (He understood and shared God's anger and disappointment.)
- 8:20-9:2 (He truly loved his people.)
- 10:6-10 (He truly loved God and acknowledged him as Lord.)
- 10:23-24 (He allowed God to teach, guide, and correct him.)
- 11:18-19 (He was focused on his mission, not on himself.)
- 12:1-4 (He brought his disappointments to God, prayed honestly.)
- 15:15 (He relied on God for strength.)
- 15:16 (He meditated on God's Word.)
- 17:14-17 (He didn't seek the approval of men.)
- 20:7-18 (He was honest with God.)
- 26:12-15 (He knew the purpose of his mission and believed in it.)
- 32:18-23 (He was familiar with and reassured by God's past faithfulness.)

Remind students that the same things that helped Jeremiah be a persistent follower of God's Word are what will help them become persistent, persevering, and committed followers of God.

Give each student a copy of **Quitters Never Win and Winners Never Quit** (page 98). Let them work on it alone for several minutes. The "Stuff to Talk About" questions at the end can be explored in small groups or as a large group. Here are those questions:

- *When/how are Christians supposed to be persistent? (Think about persistence as "doing again and again; doing early in the morning; carrying on one's shoulders" or as "running the race marked out for us.")*
- *What are some ways that you can train or prepare yourself to be a more persistent Christian? (If persistent has a negative ring for your students, use persevere or any of the words you listed in the beginning of the lesson.)*
- *Name some things in school, society, et cetera, that make persistence/perseverance/commitment difficult.*
- *In what kinds of situations are you most likely to "press on" or display persistent faith? In what kinds of situations are you most likely to lose heart or display giving-up faith? Talk about these.*

PONDER POINT - *option 2*
THE DETERMINED DEITY

The reason Jeremiah was able to persist in his role as a prophet was due in large part to the traits discussed in Ponder Point/option 1. But where did Jeremiah acquire and learn those traits? From God himself, the perfect example of persistence, dedication, and commitment—all of which are directed at us, his beloved creation.

Ask volunteers to read the following verses from Jeremiah to the group:
- 7:12, 13
- 7:22-25
- 25:3-5
- 26:2-6
- 29:19
- 32:32-33
- 35:14b-15
- 44:4-5

(All of these deal with God's persistent pursuit of human beings.)

After reading the verses above, read the following quote to your students:

"What is the Bible?...It wouldn't be enough to say that the Bible is the record of man's search for God...It is much closer to the truth to say that the Bible is the record of God's search for man. Throughout the Bible people seem bent on trying to escape from God. And in spite of this, God continues to seek after those same people, refusing to give up, continuing the pursuit..."

Robert McAfee Brown, The Bible Speaks to You, 15

Divide your students into small groups, give each group or each person a copy of **The Chase Is On!** (page 99), and ask the groups to check the character box on their sheets that you assign them. Assign them from this list:

- Adam and Eve
- Cain and Abel
- Noah, the people, and the ark
- Pharaoh and the plagues
- The Israelites in Egypt
- The Israelites worshiping the Golden Calf
- David and Bathsheba
...plus any others you want to use.

Let the groups spend 10 minutes or so thinking and talking. The discussion questions at the end of the handout can be explored in small groups or as a large group. Here are those questions:

- *Have you ever sensed God persistently pursuing you? Describe how and when you've experienced this.*
- *If you have sensed God's persistence in your life, has that affected your attitude, behavior, choices, et cetera? Explain.*
- *Do you think God pursues all people equally? Talk about why or why not.*
- *Do you think God pursues individuals throughout their entire lifetimes? Do you think God ever stops pursuing a person? Why or why not?*
- *Think about a relationship you've had that's been one-sided—you know...you've been more interested, invested more time and energy than the other person. Describe what that's like. Compare that to your relationship with God. Is it one-sided? Do you think this has any effect on God? What effect should it have on you? Explain.*

PONDER POINT - option 3
PRACTICAL PERSISTENCE AND PERSISTENT PROSE (OR, HOW A PROPHET'S PERSISTENCE HELPED WRITE A BOOK THAT WILL NEVER GO OUT OF PRINT)

Jeremiah was persistent. God is persistent. You just can't avoid the fact that persistence is important. What's more—it's a lofty goal, and lofty goals can seem unattainable.

Help your students see persistence in a concrete, focused way by looking at the story of Jeremiah, Baruch, King Jehoiakim, and the scroll found in Jeremiah 36. (Be sure to read the whole story before planning your lesson!)

> "But I don't have time to read the whole story!"
>
> Okay, no whining—Cliff's Notes to the rescue. Use the shortened version, **"Jeremiah 36: A Condensed Version"**, on page 100. You can just read it or hand out copies to your students.

Now hand out copies of **Ears for Fears** (page 101). Either in small groups or individually, have students compare the actions of different people in the Jeremiah scroll story. They'll need Bibles for looking up specific verses. The discussion questions at the end of the handout can be explored in small groups or in a large group. Here are those questions:

- *In these verses, whose response to attitude about God's Word most closely resembles your own? Explain.*
- *How does the world react to God's Word? Give examples and explain.*
- *What are some ways that people try to destroy or twist God's Word? Talk about these.*
- *Imagine that a term paper that you spent several months on was lost or destroyed. Your only option is to start at the beginning and do all the work over again. Would you tend to spend more or less time on the second paper? Devote more or less energy to it? Use more or fewer resources? Why? Read Jeremiah 36:32 for a description of Jeremiah's second project. Talk about his attitude and possible reasons for it.*

Have someone read 1 Peter 1:24, 25 to the group:

"All men are like grass, and all their glory is like the flowers of the field; the grass withers and the flowers fall, but the word of the Lord stands forever."

PAUSE

Segue into the next section, Personal Prescription, with words to this effect:

Jeremiah's determined persistence was a hallmark of his life. He learned his persistence from God himself, who never gives up on people and never stops loving people. That persistence carries over into God's Word. In Matthew 24:35, Jesus said, "Heaven and earth will pass away, but my words will never pass away." That's persistence. The same word is used in John 1:1, "In the beginning was the Word, and the Word was with God, and the Word was God." Persistence, again. When we read the Bible, we are reading the story of Jesus, a story that never gets old, about a God who never stops loving and pursuing you and me.

PERSONAL PRESCRIPTION

Give each student a copy of **Jeremiah and You, Redux** (page 102). If there's time, have them pair up and share their thoughts with another person. Encourage your students to look over their written responses on this handout during the week.

Close the lesson on a positive note (focusing on God's persistent love for them) rather than a negative note (focusing on their probable lack of persistence in seeking and following God).

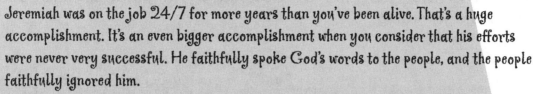

24/7

Jeremiah was on the job 24/7 for more years than you've been alive. That's a huge accomplishment. It's an even bigger accomplishment when you consider that his efforts were never very successful. He faithfully spoke God's words to the people, and the people faithfully ignored him.

Read these verses in the book of Jeremiah to find out how and why this prophet was so persistent and record what you find next to each verse. (The first verse includes an example.)

Jeremiah was able and willing to minister persistently because—

- 1:11 Jeremiah believed God was watching over circumstances

- 6:11

- 8:20-9:2

- 10:6-10

- 10:23-24

- 11:18-19

- 12:1-4

- 15:15

- 15:16

- 17:14-17

- 20:7-18

- 26:12-15

- 32:18-23

Quitters Never Win and Winners Never Quit

I have fought the good fight, I have finished the race, I have kept the faith. (2 Timothy 4:7)

Rank yourself on the following perseverance characteristics. (Be honest—it's just between you and God!) Simply make a mark (an X, your initial, a reproduction of your tattoo, whatever) somewhere along the line to indicate your rating.

	Not Really	Kinda	Now & Then	Often	Always Enthusiastically
I love God.					
I love other people.					
I acknowledge God as my Lord.					
I want God to teach and correct me.					
I keep my eyes focused on Jesus.					
I'm honest with God when I pray.					
I care more about God's approval than human approval.					
I know about the race "marked out for Christians."					
I'm running the race "marked out for Christians."					
I routinely spend time getting to know God.					
I'm familiar with God's faithfulness.					
I go to God for strength and help.					
I want to be part of God's plan for spreading the truth to others.					

Stuff to talk about:

◆When/how are Christians supposed to be persistent? (Think about persistence as "doing again and again; doing early in the morning; carrying on one's shoulders" or as "running the race marked out for us.")

◆What are some ways you can train or prepare yourself to be a more persistent Christian? (If persistent has a negative ring for you, use persevere or any of the words you listed in the beginning of the lesson.)

◆ Name some things in school or society that make persistence/perseverance/commitment/et cetera difficult.

◆In what kind of situations are you most likely to "press on" or display persistent faith? In what kind of situations are you most likely to lose heart or display giving-up faith? Talk about these.

THE CHASE IS ON!

First, check the character(s) that your group is assigned:

- Adam and Eve
- Cain and Abel
- Noah, the people, and the ark
- Pharaoh and the plagues
- The Israelites in Egypt
- The Israelites worshiping the Golden Calf
- David and Bathsheba
- Other _____

Now ask yourselves these questions and jot down your insights:

- What kind of relationship did God have with this person or persons? Good, bad, indifferent, or—?

When the person(s) disobeyed or ran away from God—

- How did God initially respond to their disobedience?

- How did God pursue these people?

- How did the people respond to God's pursuit?

Talk about these:

- Have you ever sensed God persistently pursuing you? Describe how and when you've experienced this.

- If you've sensed God's persistence in your life, has that affected your attitude, behavior, choices? Explain.

- Do you believe God pursues all people equally? Talk about why or why not.

- Do you believe God pursues individuals throughout their entire lifetimes? Do you think God ever stops pursuing a person? Explain why you think so.

- Think about a relationship you've had that's been one-sided—you know, one in which you've been more interested, invested more time and energy than the other person. Describe what that's like. Compare that to your relationship with God. Is it one-sided? Do you think this has any effect on God? Explain.

Jeremiah 36: A Condensed Version

In 605 B.C. a guy named Jehoiakim was king in Judah. He was rotten, nasty, mean, and didn't love God. Almost everyone in Judah was like the king. God still loved all those rotten, nasty, mean people, though, so he decided to give them another chance to follow him.

So God told Jeremiah, "Write down all the messages I've given you for Judah, Israel, and all the other nations. Make sure you start with my very first message. Don't skip anything. Maybe this time they'll listen to me."

Jeremiah either didn't have very neat handwriting or had a bad case of writer's cramp, so he got his friend Baruch to help him out. Jeremiah dictated. Baruch wrote. After more than a year, they finally finished.

Jeremiah wasn't allowed near the Temple, so Baruch went instead and read the book to everyone there. He went on a holiday because he figured there'd be lots of people there. He was right.

Then he read the book to some important political guys who didn't go to the Temple even on the holidays.

Then he read the book to the king, who was hanging out in his winter palace. It was December and he was keeping his royal backside warm in front of a fire. (It was a great excuse to avoid Temple services.)

When Baruch finished reading a page of the book, the king would cut out the page, rip it up, and toss it in the fire. He did this until the whole book was burned up. (He was a real jerk.)

Jeremiah said, "Bummer. And after all that hard work, too. Oh well. Didn't prophet me much, eh? Ha ha ha." (Just kidding.)

He and Baruch started over from scratch and rewrote the entire book. Without complaining.

By the way, more than 40 years later, in another country, Daniel (the lion-den guy) studied a copy of Jeremiah's book.

The End

Ears for Fears

The people in the Jeremiah scroll story had different reactions to God, to Jeremiah, and to the words in the scroll. Look up the following verses (ALL FROM JEREMIAH CHAPTER 36 UNLESS NOTED OTHERWISE) and compare "who did what" with "who did what."
(Jack cried versus Jill laughed.)

- 14-16 versus 21-23
- 5 versus 22
- 17-19 versus 26
- Daniel 9:2-3 versus 24-25
- 2 Kings 22:10-13 versus 24-25
- 2 Kings 22:18-20 versus 30-31

TALK ABOUT THESE:

- In the verses you read, whose response to attitude about God's Word most closely resembles your own? Explain.

- How does the world view and react to God's Word? Give examples and explain.

- What are some ways that people try to destroy or twist God's Word? Talk about these.

- Imagine that a term paper you spent several months on was lost or destroyed. Your only option is to start at the beginning and do all the work over again. Would you tend to spend more or less time on the second paper? Devote more or less energy to it? Use more or fewer resources? Why?

Read Jeremiah 36:32 for a description of Jeremiah's second project.
Talk about his attitude and possible reasons for it.

Jeremiah and You, Redux
(personal prescription)

Choose one of the following to think about. Jot down your insights, thoughts, and ideas. Look back at this throughout the week.

Jeremiah's persistence

● How can you become more persistent in your relationship with Christ?

● What areas do you especially need to work on?

● What one or two things most hinder you from being more persistent in your faith? What can you do to change that?

God's persistence

● How familiar are you with God's persistence?

● Are you listening to him speak to you each day? Are you aware of his presence in your life every day?

● Are you allowing him to love you unconditionally?

● What does God's persistence mean to you personally?

The Bible's persistence

● How familiar are you with God's Word?

● Do you spend time reading the story about God's pursuit of humankind? (That would be the Bible.)

● Has the Word had an impact on your life? In what ways?

● Have you introduced others to the persistent Word of God?

● Do you believe it has the power to change lives?

● How do you plan on becoming better acquainted with the Word of God?

● What part of Jeremiah's message is speaking to you? Write about it here.

EZEKIEL

(part 1)
His Wacky, Wild, Wonderful Ride

PUNDITS ✏️

Looked at one way, the book of Ezekiel is a silent tribute to his deceased wife; viewed in another way, it is an object lesson in which the prophet's personal tragedy is but a sign of larger events.

Literary Guide to the Bible, 203

Ezekiel and his contemporaries desperately needed a vision of God, as do all people whose circumstances have become their obsession and whose experience has become their dominating passion.

All Things Weird and Wonderful, 12

God has a major problem in granting visions to people. He knows they can't live with a vision of him and yet they can't live without a vision of him. So what does God do? He gradually unveils himself. He reveals enough of himself to convey an accurate picture but not so much that the receiver is completely overwhelmed.

All Things Weird and Wonderful, 12

The Jewish rabbis forbade anyone under 30 years of age to read the account of [Ezekiel's] vision. Presumably they felt that it would be too much for the sensitive spirits of their young people. This may seem amusing to us, but perhaps we should be ashamed, for we have allowed the sensitivities of our young people to be so brutalized by constant exposure to the violent and the sordid that they are capable of approaching the most overwhelming situation with nonchalance. Even God!

All Things Weird and Wonderful, 20, 21

PROFILE

- Name means "God strengthens"
- Exiled to Babylon in 597 B.C.
- Received prophetic call in April 593 B.C.
- Prophesied to complacent Jews exiled in Babylon
- Often symbolically acted out his prophecies

FROM OLD TO NEW

(where verses from this book are quoted in the New Testament) a sampling (check out the Book of Revelation for additional Ezekiel references)

Ezekiel 1:4-10 ↔ Revelation 4:8-18
Ezekiel 3:1-3 ↔ Revelation 10:9-10
Ezekiel 9:4 ↔ Revelation 7:3
Ezekiel 14:21 ↔ Revelation 6:8

Because modern minds often see humans as awesome and God as tiresome, a big dose of Ezekiel is long overdue.

Living Insights Study Bible, introduction to Ezekiel, 823

The unmistakable message of Ezekiel's life is this: There is hope when you focus on God's glory.

Living Insights Study Bible, introduction to Ezekiel, 826

Sometimes, in these days when we use Christian names freely and speak very familiarly with one another, we are tempted to treat God in the same way...the sense of wonder, mystery, and awe has diminished, and God has almost become "one of us." It is healthy, therefore, to read the Old Testament, and especially a passage like the description of Ezekiel's vision, to remind ourselves that he is God and we are human beings.

Prophets and Poets, 138

...Ezekiel—well, no one else's writings could be mistaken for that strange man's.

The Bible Jesus Read, 181

PURPOSE OF PROPHETIC PRONOUNCEMENTS

TO ENCOURAGE THE COMPLACENT, DISCOURAGED, EXILED JEWS BY DELIVERING WORDS OF JUDGMENT AND WORDS OF HOPE.

- God's glory is beyond human comprehension.
- In order to serve God, one must first "see" God.
- There's always hope when one stays focused on God.

PREVIEW

A PEEK AT THE PITH OF EZEKIEL, CHAPTERS 1-24

Ezekiel, both a prophet and priest, was called by God to speak to the discouraged and complacent Jewish exiles in Babylon. They were homesick. They were convinced that their exile would be short. And they were positive that very soon, God would deliver them home again to be near their beloved temple. Ezekiel, though, knew otherwise.

At the same time, Jeremiah was speaking to the Jews who remained behind in Judah, encouraging them to submit to Babylonian rule and be patient. Neither the Jews in Babylon nor the Jews back home liked what their particular prophet had to say. (Big surprise.)

Ezekiel's book begins with a wild vision of God—the wheels, the eyes, the faces, the wings, the creatures—that knocks Ezekiel to the ground. God stands him up and instructs him to speak to the exiled Jews. He is appointed spiritual watchman for his countrymen—a sentry on the lookout for the words of God. Ezekiel often finds himself transported to different locations where the Lord shows him visions relating to Judah's past, present, and future.

Furthermore, God frequently instructs Ezekiel to "act out" his prophecies with symbolism. Cases in point:

- He built a miniature Jerusalem, put a barrier between it and himself, and lay on his left side for 390 days as a representation of Israel's 390 years of sin. Then he lay on his right side for 40 days to represent Judah's 40 years of sin.

- He shaved his head with a sword, divided the hair into three piles, and burned one pile, scattered another pile around the city, and let the final pile blow away in the wind.
- He packed his things for a weekend getaway and left his house not through the doorway but through a hole dug with his own hands.

After warning the people extensively about their sins and the future destruction of Jerusalem, the first half of Ezekiel's book ends. And almost simultaneously, his beloved wife dies while exiled in Babylon, and his beloved temple is destroyed back home in Jerusalem.

PRECEPTS & PRINCIPLES

PRICELESS POETRY AND PROSE FROM EZEKIEL

Like the appearance of a rainbow in the clouds on a rainy day, so was the radiance around him. This was the appearance of the likeness of the glory of the Lord. When I saw it, I fell facedown..." (Ezekiel 1:28)

And you, son of man, do not be afraid of them or their words. Do not be afraid, though briers and thorns are all around you and you live among scorpions. Do not be afraid of what they say or terrified by them, though they are a rebellious house. You must speak my words to them, whether they listen or fail to listen... (2:6-7)

And he said to me, "Son of man, listen carefully and take to heart all the words I speak to you." (3:10)

The righteousness of the righteous man will be credited to him, and the wickedness of the wicked will be charged against him. (18:20b)

PLAY

BOTTOMS UP

Before the lesson, photocopy the page of slips for **Bottoms Up** (page 110)—preferably on card stock—and cut them apart. Divide into two groups. Ask for one volunteer from each group. Shuffle or otherwise mix the slips and make two piles of 10 cards each. The volunteer will describe the item on each card *from the bottom of the object or creature, up.* In other words, the clues for *giraffe* could be—
- four long legs
- legs are spotted
- short tail
- spotted body
- long neck

In other words, *long neck* cannot be the first clue. A description of the baby stroller would start with the wheels...of the apple tree, with the trunk...of the football player, with his cleats...et cetera. Time each group to see who can get all 10 cards in the shortest amount of time.

PAUSE

Segue from the description game into the Bible-study part of the lesson by saying something like this:

Sometimes it's the most common object that's the most difficult to describe to someone. So you can imagine the difficulty of describing something you had only seen once. Especially when that something is—well, just plain weird. And when it's too big to see all at once. Which is exactly what Ezekiel had to do when he saw a vision of God. The object or creature or whatever was strange, huge, and too marvelous to comprehend. The vision was so awesome, in fact, that Ezekiel fell to the ground, like a man in shock.

PONDER POINT - *option 1*
EZEKIEL'S VISION

Divide into four groups. Have each group read one of the following Scripture passages—

- Ezekiel 1:5-14
- Ezekiel 1:15:21
- Ezekiel 1:22-25
- Ezekiel 1:26-28

On blank paper, have each group list all the characteristics and descriptions included in their Scripture passage. When they're finished, have one person from each group read their passage and the list to the entire group. Ask for one-word descriptions of Ezekiel's call (*bizarre, weird, unbelievable, alien, strange,* et cetera).

Next go through the following list of characteristics and ask students for any ideas they may have about the significance or meaning of each one. Next to each characteristic, in parentheses, is a common scholarly interpretation—though by no means the only interpretation—of that characteristic.

- man face (*greatest created being*)
- lion face (*greatest wild being*)
- ox face (*greatest domestic beast*)
- eagle (*greatest bird*)
- straight legs with split hooves (*stability*)
- burnished bronze (*purity*)
- hands underneath wings (*practical hidden under the surreal*)
- touching each other (*fellowship*)
- went wherever (*availability*)
- lightning (*intensity, energy*)
- darted (*activity*)
- wheels inside wheels (*God's omnipresence—i.e., all-present*)
- awesomely tall (*God's omnipotence—all-powerful*)
- eyes (*God's omniscience—all-knowing*)

Explore these questions with your students:

- **How does Ezekiel's vision of God fit your own image of God—or not fit it? Discuss.**

- **Have you ever seen God's glory, in any sense of the word seen? Describe the circumstances.**

- **(Read to your students the quote in Pundits at the top of this lesson that begins, "The Jewish rabbis forbade..." about young people being forbidden from hearing the reading of Ezekiel's vision.) Explain why you agree or disagree with this quote. Do the Christians you know tend to view God as wild as Ezekiel did or in a more tame way? If more tame, why?**

- **What things in today's world are impressive, powerful, or awesome enough to make people "fall facedown in the dirt" (e.g., adore, be speechless, be overwhelmed with emotion, et cetera)?**

- **Has the thought of God's power and might ever made you fall face down in the dirt, in any sense of that phrase? Explain.**

A LIL' EXTRA!
Some scholars believe that Ezekiel's vision is more than just "an appearance of the likeness of the glory of the Lord" (1:28). It also depicts cherubim drawing a chariot in which God is departing from the temple in Jerusalem—a terrible thought for any Jew. The fact that the wheels moved in any and all directions, though, offered the assurance that God could go anywhere—even to Babylon, the new home of the exiles. Later on, in chapter 43, Ezekiel has a vision "that was like the visions I had seen by the Kebar River," except that in this vision, "the glory of the Lord entered the temple...and the glory of the Lord filled the temple" (43:4-5). From deepest despair to highest hope, from God's departure to God's return, from God's judgment to God's mercy, Ezekiel envisioned at all.

PONDER POINT - option 2
FATHER : GOD :: DADDY : CREATOR
(OR, FATHER IS TO GOD WHAT DADDY IS TO CREATOR)

God cannot be defined by any single word or description. He's too complex and huge to fit into any man-made categories. Sometimes the church forgets that, and we err either by presenting a God who is too out-there to be known personally, or a God who is too best friend-ish to command the respect and honor he deserves.

On a marker board, make the following chart—

	Fall facedown	**Face to face**
Parent		
Teacher		
Cop		

Explain to your students that you want them to think of examples, circumstances, or descriptions of how teens relate to parents, teachers, and cops in different ways (*fall-facedown* = honor, respect, healthy fear...*face-to-face* = friendship, conversation, hanging out).

Since the examples might be wordy, don't try to write them on the board. The chart's just for visual reference. When you've heard a few examples for each category, ask your students to vote by a show of hands on whether they view each person more often from a *fall-facedown* or *face-to-face* perspective.

Discuss the following questions—

- **Talk about the difficulties in relationships that are both fall-facedown and face-to-face. (For example, how do you transition from one to the other?)**
- **Do you think most Christians tend to have a fall-facedown, a face-to-face, or a combination relationship with God? Explain.**
- **Why/when is a person's relationship with God fall-facedown?**
- **Why/when is a person's relationship with God face-to-face?**
- **If you tend to be more fall-facedown or face-to-face, what can you do about the imbalance?**

PONDER POINT - *option 3*
EZEKIEL'S CALL

Ezekiel's encounters with God were complex. They involved a combination of his senses—hearing, seeing, tasting, feeling, touching. There are a lot of people who know *about* God, either from things they've heard or read. But *knowing* God is a very different thing. It involves intimacy, not just information.

Give each student a copy of **See God, Hear God, Know God** (page 111) and give them time to reflect and make what notes they want to. Then discuss the following with them:

- **Why do you think Ezekiel's call came after he saw and heard God? Explain.**
- **How much information or knowledge does a person need to have before being qualified to do God's work? Explain.**
- **Why do you think God told Ezekiel to be "unyielding and hardened" (Ezekiel 3:8)? Do you think there are times today when Christians need to "unyielding and hardened"? Explain.**
- **What does it mean to "take to heart all the words" God speaks to you (Ezekiel 3:10)? Talk about some of the ways you can do this.**

PAUSE

Segue to the next section, Personal Prescription, by saying something like this:

The book of Ezekiel—especially his vision recorded early in his book—seems pretty weird to a lot of people. But it's much deeper than that. It shows us God's majesty, mystery, and hugeness—his outside-the-box-ness. Until we personally grapple with these unbelievable characteristics of God, we cannot really hear nor understand him accurately. God doesn't want us to have a one-sided or narrow view of him. He wants us to know him—all of him.

PERSONAL PRESCRIPTION

The point of this activity is to help your kids see God more fully. If you can, play worship music during this activity—particularly a song that highlights God's character and sovereignty.

Say something like this—and don't rush it. Let this take five minutes or more, if your students are with you:

While the music plays, close your eyes and meditate on God's awesome glory, majesty, and power...Listen to the music...Listen to the silence...Listen to the Holy Spirit...Look at God in your mind...
Remember anything you "heard" or "saw" while you focused on God...if you want, write it down when you get home, while it's still fresh in your mind.

PRAYER

Have volunteers from the group pray phrases that acknowledge God's glory and majesty. For example, "God, you are awesome...God, you are powerful...God, you are pure." Then close with a prayer like this:

God, we want to see your glory in such a way that we fall facedown on the ground. Help us not forget that even though you are our loving Daddy, you are also the creator and ruler of the universe. Amen.

THE LION, THE WITCH, AND THE WARDROBE...

...by C.S. Lewis contains a great example of the need to enlarge one's view of God's greatness.

Read your kids chapter 8 from, "Oh, yes! Tell us about Aslan!" through "'I'm longing to see him,' said Peter, 'even if I do feel frightened when it comes to the point.'" The lion Aslan is seen by many readers to be a Christ figure.

Slips for the activity **Bottoms Up** in the Ezekiel lesson (part 1). Photocopy this page, cut apart, and follow the instructions in the activity description on page 105.

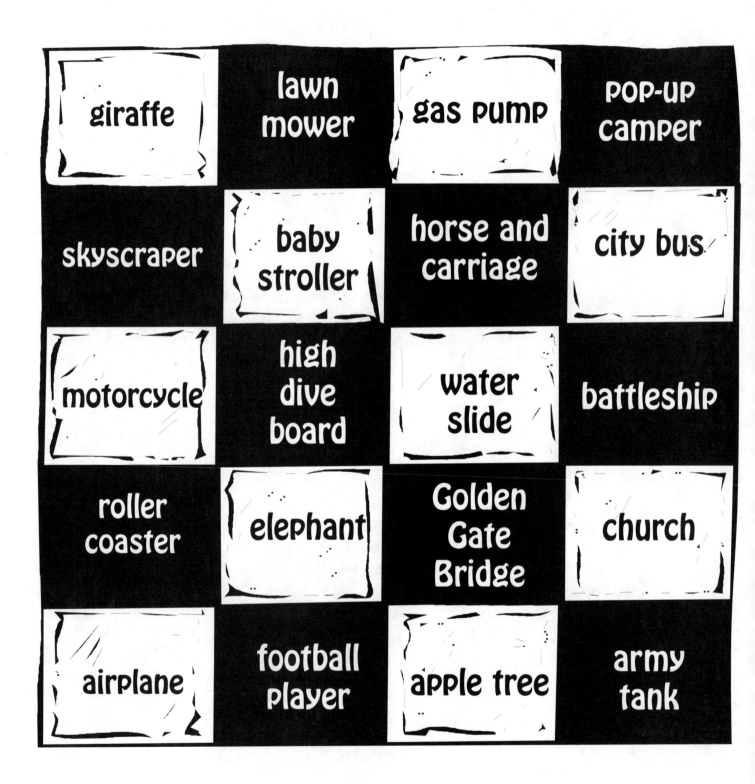

giraffe

lawn mower

gas pump

POP-UP camper

skyscraper

baby stroller

horse and carriage

city bus

motorcycle

high dive board

water slide

battleship

roller coaster

elephant

Golden Gate Bridge

church

airplane

football player

apple tree

army tank

See God, Hear God, Know God

First Ezekiel saw God (Ezekiel 1:4-28).
Then Ezekiel heard God (2:1-8).
Then Ezekiel ate (or "took in") Scripture (2:9-3:3).
Then Ezekiel personalized (or followed) Scripture (3:10).
Finally, Ezekiel went out to do God's work (the whole book!)

Think about times that you've heard God speak to you or call to you (audibly or not) through the following means. Then think about what God said in those instances. Write down the things that come to mind.

If God spoke to me, it was through—(check one or more)
- ⬭ a speaker or teacher
- ⬭ Scripture
- ⬭ music
- ⬭ something I saw
- ⬭ silence
- ⬭ other _____
- ⬭ I'm not aware of God ever speaking to me

This is what I heard God say to me:

EZEKIEL
(part 2)
A Bony Sequel

PUNDITS 🖉

Many of the Lord's people don't like to think about the obvious bone yard in which they live, whether it is their church or their community, but God wants them to be aware of it. He will give a personal guided tour to any who will allow his hand to be upon them.

All Things Weird and Wonderful, 133

Preaching the Word in the power of the Spirit will not only make bones into skeletons, but skeletons into corpses, corpses into people, and people into armies.

All Things Weird and Wonderful, 134

Be careful that you don't underestimate the power of the God of the universe. Nothing is impossible with God! If God can put muscle and flesh on dry bones and build a body out of them, surely he can renew someone you might think is all washed up and finished in God's sight.

Living Insights Study Bible,
introduction to Ezekiel, 826

PROFILE

- Was commanded by God not to mourn his wife's death

- Final prophecy in July 571 B.C.

- Called "son of man" by God 93 times

- Source of a familiar phrase to many Christians, stand in the gap (22:30)

- Know God is recurring theme in book

PURPOSE OF PROPHETIC PRONOUNCEMENTS

TO ENCOURAGE THE COMPLACENT, DISCOURAGED, EXILED JEWS BY DELIVERING WORDS OF JUDGMENT AND WORDS OF HOPE.

- God's glory is beyond human comprehension.
- In order to serve God, one must first "see" God.
- There's always hope when one stays focused on God.

FROM OLD TO NEW

(where verses from this book are quoted in the New Testament) a sampling (check out the Book of Revelation for additional Ezekiel references)

Ezekiel 20:41 ↔ 2 Corinthians 6:17
Ezekiel 27:27-32 ↔ Revelation 18:13-19
Ezekiel 36:22 ↔ Romans 2:24
Ezekiel 37:27 ↔ 2 Corinthians 6:16

Near the beginning of Ezekiel, God tells the prophet to be both a watchtower for Israel and a mouthpiece for God, who adds this: "I will make your tongue stick to the roof of your mouth so that you will be silent and unable to rebuke them..." (Ezekiel 3:26) Talk about mixed signals. God said speak. Then God said silence. God didn't want Ezekiel to speak until he'd heard that the enemy had conquered Jerusalem, the homeland.

The first half of Ezekiel ends with his beloved wife's death. Back home in Judah, God's beloved city Jerusalem is on the verge of her own death and destruction at the hands of the Babylonians. Ezekiel's pain and sorrow reflect God's pain and sorrow. After an eight-chapter intermission (25-32) of messages to foreign nations and rulers, the second half of Ezekiel begins much like the first.

In chapter 33, God again calls Ezekiel to be a watchman for his people—but this time, when God says speak, he doesn't follow it with silence (33:22). Even though circumstances back in Judah seem flooded with despair, Ezekiel is now instructed to communicate hope, not judgment, to the people. He gives them pictures of new life, restored glory, and eternal peace. Chapters 38 and 39, which seem to veer off track, are thought by some scholars to have been inserted at a later date. The last eight chapters give an extensive description of a new and restored temple, filled with the glory of the Lord.

KEEPING THE CANCER AS WELL AS THE CURE

Does the silencing/speaking of Ezekiel have anything to say to today's evangelists, teachers, and ministers of the gospel?

It used to be that new converts were ushered into the kingdom of God via hellfire and brimstone. The terror-inducing question, "Do you know where you're going if you die right now?" was enough to scare some folks into a saving faith. Too bad they weren't as well acquainted with God's love, grace, forgiveness, and mercy.

Lately, though, it seems like the pendulum might be swinging to the other extreme. God is presented as a loving, kind, good, forgiving, and merciful cure for the sinsick and lost. But what good is a cure or answer if you don't know the disease or question?

We must not fall into the trap of presenting either of these extreme gospels. Ezekiel demonstrates that there's a good rationale for keeping silent about the cure (salvation, redemption, new life, restored relationship with God) until the disease (sinful self-centeredness) and the question (how can a person be in right relationship with God?) are presented. After all, can a cured people fully appreciate the miracle of their restoration to health without also fully realizing the severity and terminal condition of their disease?

PRECEPTS & PRINCIPLES
POETRY AND PROSE FROM EZEKIEL: THE SEQUEL

Say to them, "As surely as I live," declares the Sovereign Lord, "I take no pleasure in the death of the wicked, but rather that they turn from their ways and live" (Ezekiel 33:11a).

If a righteous man turns from his righteousness and does evil, he will die for it. And if a wicked man turns away from his wickedness and does what is just and right, he will live by doing so. (33:18, 19)

For this is what the Sovereign Lord says: "I myself will search for my sheep and look after them. As a shepherd looks after his scattered flock when he is with them, so will I look after my sheep. I will rescue them from all the places where they were scattered on a day of clouds and darkness" (34:11-12).

"You my sheep, the sheep of my pasture, are people, and I am your God," declares the Sovereign Lord. (34:31)

"I will sprinkle clean water on you, and you will be clean; I will cleanse you from all your impurities and from all your idols. I will give you a new heart and put a new spirit in you; I will remove from you your heart of stone and give you a heart of flesh. And I will put my Spirit in you and move you to follow my decrees and be careful to keep my laws" (36:25-27).

PLAY

Divide the group in half. Have each half form concentric circles facing one another. When the music starts, each circle moves to its right, passing by one another in opposite directions. When the music stops, you call out one of these body/bone combinations:

- **heel/elbow**
- **elbow/shoulder**
- **knee/foot**
- **foot/head**
- **head/foot**
- **hand/ear**
- **ear/ankle**
- **big toe/thumb**
- **shoulder/shoulder**
- **elbow/ear**

…and you can make up combinations as needed.

For instance, when the music stops, you can call out "Heel/elbow!" at which point the person in the outside circle touches her heel to the elbow of the player in the inner circle. Then the music starts up, circles begin rotating again, and the process repeats itself.

PAUSE

Segue from this goofy game to the Bible-study part of the lesson with words to this effect:

God created our bodies according to a specific plan, and putting elbows into ears probably isn't part of the program. Human beings are amazing creations, from the skeleton to the muscles to the skin to the senses. Though we all die eventually, God designed us to first live—both physically and spiritually.

PONDER POINT - *option 1*
MOSTLY DEAD

Show the scene from *The Princess Bride* in which the supposedly dead Wesley is brought to Miracle Max (Billy Crystal), who proclaims him "only mostly dead." (1:09:48—1:14:25) Then say something like this:

Many people today feel dried up, discouraged, maybe even "mostly dead." We're going to look at what God can do for those people if they trust him.

Have one or several students read Ezekiel 37:1-14 to the group. Give this background:

Ezekiel was a prophet to the exiled Jews in Babylon. After being removed from their homeland and forced to live in a new country with strange customs and laws, the people were feeling discouraged and abandoned by God. After hearing that Jerusalem, the hometown they'd been forced to leave several years earlier, had now been totally destroyed by the enemy, the people were even more despondent. Their hopes and dreams for someday returning home were dashed. Ezekiel's vision of dry bones was intended to give them hope and encouragement.

After reading the Scripture, divide into groups of about five. Give each group or each student a copy of **Mostly Dead** (page 120) and allow several minutes for them to work on it. When the groups are finished, regather, and ask each group to read aloud what items make them feel the "most dead." Then discuss the following:

- *Describe why the things on your list make you feel "mostly dead."*
- *What emotions do you experience when your spirit feels slightly wounded? Deeply wounded?*
- *How do these experiences and emotions affect the way you view and feel about yourself? Talk about this.*
- *Do you think typical American values cause people to feel "mostly alive" or "mostly dead"? Explain.*

PONDER POINT - *option 2*
"IT'S JUST A FLESH WOUND!"

 Show the clip in *Monty Python and the Holy Grail* where King Arthur duels with the Black Knight, who never does admit defeat even when Arthur's sword lops off his arms and legs: "It's only a flesh wound!" he exclaims. The Black Knight's sense of well-being and physical health is hideously distorted. (13:43—16:35)

There are a lot of ways to deal with feeling "mostly dead." Just check out TV commercials, the countless health and beauty products you see wherever you turn, the shelves of self-help books in Borders or Barnes & Noble. For those who want to feel "mostly better," cures range from compulsive shopping to shutting out the world, from driving around town to getting drunk or high.

On a marker board, make two columns, one titled CURES FOR THE PARTLY DEAD (temporary bad feelings, et cetera) and CURES FOR THE MOSTLY DEAD (deeper, more severe and lasting problems). Ask your students to brainstorm about ways that people try to get rid of their "partly dead" and "mostly dead" feelings on their own. Here are some examples of cures if you need to jumpstart the discussion:

- shop
- eat
- listen to music

- watch TV
- sit alone in room
- write in journal
- drink
- talk on the phone
- hate parents
- get revenge
- run away from home
- suicide

After creating the two lists, have a student read Ezekiel 37:1-3 aloud. Then have volunteers read the following verses that deal with sickness, cures, and life:

- Matthew 9:10-13
- John 4:13
- John 5:24
- Psalm 147:3
- Matthew 16:25
- Psalm 116:1-6

Discuss the following:

- *What are some of the ways that God heals our feelings of being "mostly dead?"*
- *When you're feeling discouraged, hurt, or "mostly dead," where or to whom do you usually go for help?*
- *What is the world's opinion of people who turn to God for help with being "mostly dead"? Explain.*
- *In a single phrase, what is the world's advice to those who feel "mostly dead?" What "cures, remedies, prescriptions" does the world offer?*

PONDER POINT - *option 3*
FULLY ALIVE

 The only way that "mostly dead" dry bones can become fully alive is through God's power. Have one student read Ezekiel 37:4 and another read Ezekiel 37:14. Give each student a copy of **Fully Alive** (page 121). After they work on it a few minutes, regather as a large group and ask for volunteers to share one or two of their responses. Then discuss questions like these:

- *How does God's Word act as a supernatural skeleton? (i.e., it gives you a support system, holds you upright, holds you together, et cetera) Explain. What about the other items in your skeleton list?*
- *How does God cover you and act as supernatural skin? (i.e., he forgives, he loves, he's patient, et cetera) Explain.*
- *Let's say your supernatural skin is visible to others, just like your physical skin. What do you want the world to notice when they see your supernatural skin? Explain.*

- *How have you personally experienced God's protective covering? Explain.*
- *How does God fill you up and act as supernatural spirit? (i.e., he teaches truth, he reveals wonder, he relates and converses, et cetera) Explain.*
- *Is it possible to have only a supernatural skeleton, only supernatural skin, or only a supernatural spirit and still be an alive Christian? Why or why not? Explain the relationship between the three—that is, how do they work together?*

PAUSE

Segue into the next section, Personal Prescription, by saying something like this:

People spend a lot of time, energy, and money trying to make themselves feel more alive and less "mostly dead." Some of those cures may work for a while, but eventually their potency wears off, and we're back right where we started...feeling "mostly dead." The only thing that can cure us from "mostly deadness" is God—big doses of God. It's not enough to just believe in him; then we're just skeletons. It's not enough to acknowledge his love and kindness; then we're just skeletons with skin. We need a supernatural skeleton, skin, and spirit.

PERSONAL PRESCRIPTION - option 1

Give all students a copy of **Take Regularly to Feel Fully Alive** (page 122) for them to complete, either individually or in small groups.

PERSONAL PRESCRIPTION - option 2

Give each student a copy of **Before and After** (page 123) to think about and complete either individually or in small groups. Students can discuss the "More..." questions either in small groups or as a large, regathered group. Here are those questions:

Nuj' erz

Dry bones = dead bones
There wasn't a single un-dry bone in the bunch
"Dry" means lacking water
Jesus = living water
Jesus is cure for dry bones
Dry bones didn't stay that way
Reborn bones look and act differently than dry bones
Bones plus skin doesn't equal life
"Breath entered them; they came to life"

- *Does my AC ["after Christ"] life look significantly different from my BC ["before Christ"] life? Is so, why? If not, why?*
- *How would I like to see my AC life change and mature?*
- *What can I do to help make that possible?*

PRAYER

 Break into small groups. Tell students to thank God for ways that he has brought them back to life. Then end with something like this:

Dear God,
We don't want to be a valley of dry, "mostly dead" bones. We want to experience real life. We want to be filled with your spirit so that we're able to stand strong as we face the world. Show us how to rely on you, not ourselves, for a full life. Amen.

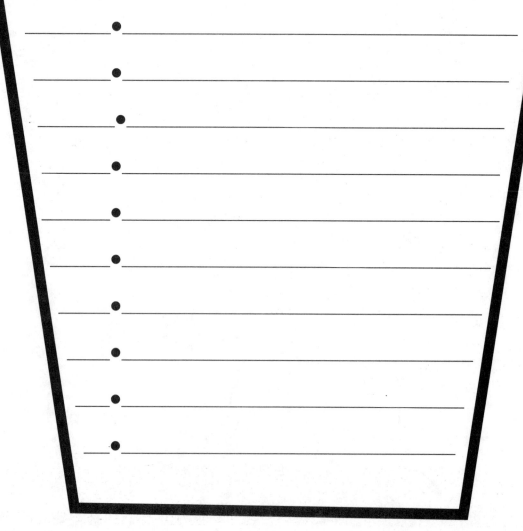

MOSTLY DEAD

God's diagnosis of the Israelites was that they were dead. This was true spiritually, but also emotionally—especially after hearing about the destruction of their home-land. Because there was still hope, however—and with God there is always hope—one might say the Israelites were only mostly dead.

Make a list of 10 or so things that make you feel "mostly dead"—you know, like failing a test, getting cut from a team, having your parents split up, et cetera. List them to the right of each bullet.

Now, on the line to the left of each bulleted item, rate the negative intensity of each by assigning a number from 1 to 10 (1 = makes me feel only a little dead, discouraged, disappointed, or upset; and 10 = makes me feel hugely dead, crushed, depressed, despondent, helpless, and hopeless).

Fully Alive

It takes three things to be fully alive:

> Skeleton (support, root system, shape)
> Skin (protective covering)
> Spirit ("image of God"-ness, being human)

List some things below that provide a Christian with a skeleton (inside the sil-houette), skin (outside the silhouette) and spirit (in the heart).

Take Regularly to Feel Fully Alive

Think about Ezekiel's vision of dry bones and his statement that in order for dry and "mostly dead" bones to come alive, God would have to be involved. Now think about the three parts of a fully alive Christian. Beside each one, write one or two ways that you can take larger doses of each so that you can experience real life more fully.

Skeleton *(e.g., God's truth and foundation)*:

Skin *(e.g., God's love, forgiveness, protection)*:

Spirit *(e.g., God's joy, kindness, hope)*:

Before and After
(personal prescription)

There are lots of ways to describe the difference between a person's life before and after becoming a Christian:

I once was lost but now am found...
I once was blind but now can see...
I once was dead but now am alive.

Think about your life before knowing Christ. Then think about your current life with Christ. Below, compare your BC (before Christ) life with your AC (after Christ) life by listing the characteristics of both.

(If you've been a Christian for a long time, compare your early AC life to your present AC life. If you know about Christ but haven't yet decided to begin a relationship with him, fill in the BC column. Then think about what an AC life might be like. Is it a life you'd like to have? It's yours for the taking...)

MY BC LIFE	*MY AC LIFE*

More...

- Does my AC life look significantly different from my BC life? Is so, why? If not, why?

- How would I like to see my AC life change and mature?

- What can I do to help make that possible?

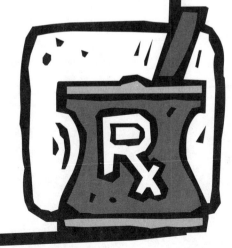

HAGGAI & ZECHARIAH

Coaches with Different Styles

PUNDITS

Haggai urged the Judeans to rebuild the temple, not in order to earn the favor of the Lord...Rather, Haggai urged the people to rebuild the temple as the outward sign of their renewed inner devotion to God.

Preaching from the Minor Prophets, 105

Pictured in this passage [Haggai] are a people who resemble much of American society. They are a busy people, but they concern themselves only with their own self-interest.

Preaching from the Minor Prophets, 106

God (through Zechariah) intended that the apocalyptic material combined with the judgment and salvation oracles should function as an encouragement to his people to complete the rebuilding of his temple.

Zondervan NIV Commentary, 1515

...[Zechariah sees] in the temple a symbol of God's involvement in the world. It is the place where heaven and earth intersect, where we have glimpses through the gates of heaven.

Prophets and Poets, 288

PROFILE
ZECHARIAH

- Began prophesying two months after Haggai finished prophesying
- Encouraged, motivated, and inspired Jews to finish the new temple
- Received apocalyptic visions of coming Messiah and New Jerusalem
- Returned to Jerusalem in 538 B.C.
- Was a prophet and priest
- Born in Babylon during exile
- Name means "the Lord remembers"

PROFILE
HAGGAI

- Prophesied for only four months, from August through December, 520 B.C.
- Name means "feast or festal"
- Probably returned to Jerusalem in 538 B.C. from Babylonian exile
- Was probably older than 70 when he prophesied
- Against all odds as a prophet, he was actually listened to and obeyed by people
- Exhorted, challenged, and held Jews accountable for finishing the new temple

FROM OLD TO NEW
(where verses from this book are quoted in the New Testament)

Haggai 2:6 ↔ Hebrews 12:26
Haggai 2:3-4 ↔ Hebrews 10:37-38
Zechariah 3:2 ↔ Jude 9
Zechariah 4:1-2 ↔ Revelation 11:4
Zechariah 6:1-6 ↔ Revelation 6:2-8
Zechariah 8:16 ↔ Ephesians 4:25
Zechariah 9:9 ↔ Matthew 21:5, John 12:15
Zechariah 11:13 ↔ Matthew 27:9-10
Zechariah 12:10 ↔ John 19:37, Revelation 1:7
Zechariah 13:7 ↔ Matthew 26:31, Mark 14:27

PURPOSE OF PROPHETIC PRONOUNCEMENTS
TO ENCOURAGE GOD'S PEOPLE TO REBUILD HIS TEMPLE

- Examine your priorities, put God first. (Haggai)
- Look to God's promises for vision, motivation, and inspiration to do his work. (Zechariah)
- Finish what you start. (Both)

PREVIEW
A PEEK AT THE PITH OF HAGGAI AND ZECHARIAH

A history lesson:
- In 605 B.C., Babylon invaded Judah and deported a group of young nobles, including Daniel.
- Jehoikim was made king of Judah but was nothing more than a puppet ruler for Babylon.
- Jehoikim rebelled against Babylon's control of Judah.
- In 598, Babylon attacked and reclaimed Judah.
- The next year Judah surrendered and many Jews were exiled to Babylon.
- Ten years later Jerusalem (the capital of Judah) was taken captive by Babylon. The walls and temple were destroyed. Most of the remaining Jews were exiled to Babylon.
- Fifty years later, in 538 B.C., the exiled Jews were allowed to return home. Some returned to Judah, others stayed in what had become home by then, Babylon.
- The Jews began to rebuild the temple, but quickly got tired and quit.
- In 520, Haggai and Zechariah came on the scene. In four prophecies, Haggai said, "How dare you build your own houses and take care of your own interests while ignoring God's temple! Get back to work on it!"
- Two months later, Zechariah picked up the theme and said, "Don't you know that the new temple will be a place to glorify God? It will be a symbol of our relationship with him. I know you're tired and discouraged. Look to God for the strength to finish. You can do it!"

PRECEPTS & PRINCIPLES
PRICELESS POETRY AND PROSE FROM HAGGAI AND ZECHARIAH

Now this is what the Lord Almighty says: "Give careful thought to your ways" (Haggai 1:5).

Then Haggai, the Lord's messenger, gave this message of the Lord to the people: "I am with you," declares the Lord. (Haggai 1:13)

"You expected much, but see, it turned out to be little. What you brought home, I blew away. Why?" declares the Lord Almighty. "Because of my house, which remains a ruin, while each of you is busy with his own house" (Haggai 1:9).

Therefore tell the people: "This is what the Lord Almighty says: 'Return to me,' declares the Lord Almighty, 'and I will return to you,' says the Lord Almighty" (Zechariah 1:3).

"Shout and be glad, O Daughter of Zion. For I am coming, and I will live among you," declares the Lord. (Zechariah 2:10)

"Not by might nor by power, but by my Spirit," says the Lord Almighty. (Zechariah 4:6b)

Rejoice greatly, O Daughter of Zion! Shout, Daughter of Jerusalem! See, your king comes to you, righteous and having salvation, gentle and riding on a donkey, on a colt, the foal of a donkey. (Zechariah 9:9)

PLAY - *option 1*
SAM-I-AM VERSUS SAM-I-AM-NOT

Divide your group into teams of five or six. Give each group a copy of **Sam-I-Am versus Sam-I-Am-Not** (page 131). Explain that Sam-I-Am (from *Green Eggs and Ham*) was a great motivator. He never gave up. He kept pushing until his goal was accomplished. Motivation comes in two forms—"Try it, you'll like it" (the Sam-I-Am column) and "Eat it because it's good for you" (Sam-I-Am-Not column). Give the teams about five minutes to fill in their answers. Then have each team read their responses to the entire group. If any other group has the same response, both teams must cross it off. When all the teams have given their answers, add up the totals. The teams with the most answers wins.

PLAY - *option 2*
RAPPIN' SEUSS

Have a kid, group of kids, or leader read *Green Eggs and Ham* accompanied by a rap beat. Use a keyboard's drum program or a karaoke machine or just a CD. Or if you've got drummers in your group, let them provide the rhythm. It's funny and entertaining. If a group performs, vote on best performance. Stage a competition between two readers or groups by alternating pages in the book. Be creative!

PAUSE

Segue from Seuss to the Scripture lesson by saying something like this:

When you're trying to do a job or complete a project, it helps to have someone cheering you on and providing encouragement. Sometimes this encouragement is stern, like the Sam-I-Am-Not examples. Sometimes it's inspiring, like the Sam-I-Am examples. Both kinds of encouragement are good and effective. Two prophets in the Bible, Haggai and Zechariah, had to encourage a group a people to finish rebuilding God's temple, a job the people started—and stopped—years earlier.

PONDER POINT - option 1
HAGGAI, THE SAM-I-AM-NOT PROPHET (AN INTENSE MOTIVATOR)

Haggai spent four months encouraging the Jews to rebuild the temple. He realized that the people had become indifferent and apathetic about the project. They were preoccupied with their own projects and interest. His goal was to shake them up, wake them up, and get them moving in the right direction. One of the ways he did this was by challenging them to examine their priorities.

Give each student a copy of **Give Careful Thought to...** (page 132). Let them work on it in pairs. Then regather and discuss these ideas:

- *Some people make a conscious effort to prioritize their time and activities. Others just take things as they come. What kind of person are you? Talk about this.*
- *Talk about the process of setting priorities. Is it easy? Does it work out the way you plan? What things are helpful in doing this? What are the biggest challenges?*
- *How do you determine what your priorities are? Talk about this.*
- *In order to set priorities, you need to have a gauge, a yardstick, or some kind of meter to measure the importance, value, and immediacy of things. Talk about how you do this in your life, or how you've seen others do it.*

Now have someone read Haggai 1:2-11 to the group. Point out the misplaced priorities of the Jews in verses 2-4 and 9: "God, you'll have to wait your turn. We're taking care of our own business right now."
Then ask these questions:

- *Why, when, and where do you put God on hold while you take care of your own business?*
- *Who or what encourages you to straighten out your priorities?*

PONDER POINT - option 2
ZECHARIAH, THE SAM-I-AM PROPHET (AN INSPIRING ENCOURAGER)

Zechariah inspired the people to finish rebuilding by giving them a vision of what the completed temple would represent.
On a whiteboard, write the following three phrases:

- A SYMBOL OF GOD'S GLORY AND POWER
- A REMINDER OF THE COMING MESSIAH
- A SYMBOL OF GOD'S RELATIONSHIP WITH HIS PEOPLE

Divide students into small groups. Assign one of the following Scriptures to each group. Depending on attendance, you may have more than one group per Scripture.

- Zechariah 8:1-7
- Zechariah 8:8-13

WANNA DATE?

The four prophecies Haggai delivered to Judah (see Preview) can be accurately dated—and these dates are, believe it or not, widely agreed upon among scholars:

1:1-11	August 29, 520 B.C.
1:12-15	September 21
1:15-2:9	October 17
2:10, 20-23	December 18

- Zechariah 8:14-19
- Zechariah 8:20-23
- Zechariah 9:9-13

Tell them to read the Scripture and look for examples of the three items listed on the whiteboard, which are ways that Zechariah encouraged and inspired the people. (For example, 8:3 reminds the people that the finished temple will be God's dwelling place. And 8:7 reminds the people of their relationship with God.)

When the groups have finished, gather together and ask for a few examples. Then discuss the following:

- *Talk about a time when you received inspiring encouragement from someone. What did they say or do to help you?*
- *Talk about a time, past or present, when you could have used some inspiring encouragement but didn't get it. What happened as a result?*

PONDER POINT - *option 3*

Haggai and Zechariah had different "coaching styles," but they had the same message: *Rebuild the temple!* But what does a Jerusalem temple from 520 B.C. have to do with us today?

Let's look at where God had been in the habit of meeting his people:
- According to Exodus 24, Moses met with God on Mt. Sinai.
- According to Exodus 25, God instructed the people to build a Tabernacle for him to dwell in.
- According to Exodus 33, Moses met with God in a "tent of meeting."
- According to 1 Kings 5, Solomon began building a temple for the Lord.
- According to the books of Haggai and Zechariah, the temple was rebuilt.
- In A.D. 70 the Romans destroyed the rebuilt temple.

Which brings us back to the same question: *What does a Jerusalem temple from 520 B.C. have to do with us today?*

The temple has always been where God dwelt and met with his people. It was "a symbol of God's involvement in the world. It is the place where heaven and earth intersect, where we have glimpses through the gates of heaven" (*Prophets and Poets*, 288).

Have your students brainstorm characteristics, features, and purposes of a temple. List these on a whiteboard. Then use the following Scriptures to see what the New Testament says about temples:
- Acts 17:24
- 1 Corinthians 3:16-17
- 1 Corinthians 6:19-20
- 2 Corinthians 6:16
- Ephesians 2:19-22

Furthermore, today's "temple," according to the New Testament, is the body of Christ. Each Christian dwells in a body that's called "the temple of God." Discuss these ideas—

> ### DIFFERENT TACTICS, SAME GOAL
> Show a pair of clips from the movie **"Remember the Titans"** that exemplify two different coaching styles. (49:10-51:51) Both styles had same goal—victory—but used different tactics.

- *If you are a Christian, you are God's temple. What message, then, does Haggai and Zechariah have for you today?*
- *What implications does this have (knowing that you are God's temple) for your daily life? Your decision-making? Your activities?*

PAUSE

 Segue to the next section, Personal Prescription, with words to this effect:

Haggai and Zechariah's message is relevant for today. If you are God's temple, then these two prophets are encouraging you to give your temple the attention it needs. You must maintain God's dwelling place—that is, your heart, mind, body, and soul. You must continually build on them and be good to them—and you will grow as a Christian!

To accomplish this, remember Haggai and Zechariah. Keep your priorities straight. And keep your eye on God's promise and purpose regarding your life both now and in the future.

PERSONAL PRESCRIPTION
TEMPLE INVENTORY

 Give each student a copy of **Temple Inventory** (page 133). Let them have several minutes to think about it. Then have them pair up with another student and share one or two of their answers. When they've finished, have them pray together about the things they've learned and discussed.

Sam-I-Am versus Sam-I-Am-Not

For each Green Eggs and Ham task below, come up with as many examples as you can of both Sam-I-Am and Sam-I-Am-Not motivations.

Green Eggs and Ham tasks	Sam-I-Am examples	Sam-I-Am-Not examples
Clean your room	Think of all the neat things you'll find under the rubble You'll be able to see your new carpeting	Or you'll be grounded on Saturday The neighbors are complaining about the smell
Finish your homework		
Take out the trash		

Give Careful Thought to...

Relationships

Think of the four most important relationships you have. Divide the pie chart into 4 sections, size them according to the importance of the relationship (bigger for more important, smaller for less important), and label each section with the specific relationship

Time

Think about how you spend your time each day. Divide the pie chart into 4 to 7 sections, size them according to the amount of time you spend on each activity (bigger for more time, smaller for less time), and label each section with the specific activity.

Now look at your two charts.

- Is the relationship that's most important to you the one that you spend the most time on?

- Is the activity you spend the most time on the activity that's most important to you?

Temple Inventory
(personal prescription)

You are God's temple. You are God's dwelling place. So in what condition is your temple? (body, mind, spirit, heart, soul)

Describe your temple's foundation. What is it made of? What does it look like? How strong is it?

Describe what others see when they look at your temple. How sturdy is it? How well is it maintained? What's the interior like?

Think of one or two specific ways you can work on "building" or "rebuilding" your temple this week. Write them here and keep this as a reminder of how important God's temple is.

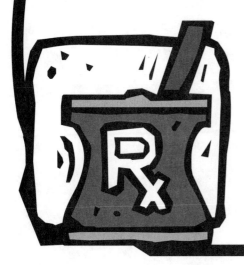

Resources from Youth Specialties
www.youthspecialties.com

Ideas Library
Ideas Library on CD-ROM 2.0
Administration, Publicity, & Fundraising
Camps, Retreats, Missions, & Service Ideas
Creative Meetings, Bible Lessons, & Worship Ideas
Crowd Breakers & Mixers
Discussion & Lesson Starters
Discussion & Lesson Starters 2
Drama, Skits, & Sketches
Drama, Skits, & Sketches 2
Drama, Skits, & Sketches 3
Games
Games 2
Games 3
Holiday Ideas
Special Events

Bible Curricula
Backstage Pass to the Bible Kit
Creative Bible Lessons from the Old Testament
Creative Bible Lessons in 1 & 2 Corinthians
Creative Bible Lessons in Galatians and Philippians
Creative Bible Lessons in John
Creative Bible Lessons in Romans
Creative Bible Lessons on the Life of Christ
Creative Bible Lessons on the Prophets
Creative Bible Lessons in Psalms
Wild Truth Bible Lessons
Wild Truth Bible Lessons 2
Wild Truth Bible Lessons—Pictures of God
Wild Truth Bible Lessons—Pictures of God 2
Wild Truth Bible Lessons—Dares from Jesus

Topical Curricula
Creative Junior High Programs from A to Z, Vol. 1 (A-M)
Creative Junior High Programs from A to Z, Vol. 2 (N-Z)
Girls: 10 Gutsy, God-Centered Sessions
        on Issues That Matter to Girls
Guys: 10 Fearless, Faith-Focused Sessions
        on Issues That Matter to Guys
Good Sex
The Justice Mission
Live the Life! Student Evangelism Training Kit
The Next Level Youth Leader's Kit
Roaring Lambs
So What Am I Gonna Do with My Life?
Student Leadership Training Manual
Student Underground
Talking the Walk
What Would Jesus Do? Youth Leader's Kit
Wild Truth Bible Lessons
Wild Truth Bible Lessons 2
Wild Truth Bible Lessons—Pictures of God
Wild Truth Bible Lessons—Pictures of God 2
Wild Truth Bible Lessons—Dares from Jesus

Discussion Starters
Discussion & Lesson Starters (Ideas Library)
Discussion & Lesson Starters 2 (Ideas Library)
EdgeTV
Every Picture Tells a Story
Get 'Em Talking
Keep 'Em Talking!
Good Sex Drama
Have You Ever...?
Name Your Favorite
Unfinished Sentences
What If...?
Would You Rather...?
High School TalkSheets—Updated!
More High School TalkSheets—Updated!
High School TalkSheets from Psalms
        and Proverbs—Updated!
Junior High-Middle School TalkSheets—Updated!
More Junior High-Middle School TalkSheets—Updated!
Junior High-Middle School TalkSheets from Psalms
        and Proverbs—Updated!
Real Kids Ultimate Discussion-Starting Videos:
        Castaways
        Growing Up Fast
        Hardship & Healing
        Quick Takes
        Survivors
        Word on the Street
Small Group Qs

Drama Resources
Drama, Skits, & Sketches (Ideas Library)
Drama, Skits, & Sketches 2 (Ideas Library)
Drama, Skits, & Sketches 3 (Ideas Library)
Dramatic Pauses
Good Sex Drama
Spontaneous Melodramas
Spontaneous Melodramas 2
Super Sketches for Youth Ministry

Game Resources
Games (Ideas Library)
Games 2 (Ideas Library)
Games 3 (Ideas Library)
Junior High Game Nights
More Junior High Game Nights
Play It!
Screen Play CD-ROM

Additional Programming Resources
(also see Discussion Starters)
The Book of Uncommon Prayer
Camps, Retreats, Missions, & Service Ideas
        (Ideas Library)
Creative Meetings, Bible Lessons, & Worship Ideas
        (Ideas Library)
Crowd Breakers & Mixers (Ideas Library)
Everyday Object Lessons
Great Fundraising Ideas for Youth Groups
More Great Fundraising Ideas for Youth Groups
Great Retreats for Youth Groups
Great Talk Outlines for Youth Ministry

Holiday Ideas (Ideas Library)
Incredible Questionnaires for Youth Ministry
Kickstarters
Memory Makers
Special Events (Ideas Library)
Videos That Teach
Videos That Teach 2
Worship Services for Youth Groups

Quick Question Books
Have You Ever...?
Name Your Favorite
Unfinished Sentences
What If...?
Would You Rather...?

Videos & Video Curricula
Dynamic Communicators Workshop
EdgeTV
The Justice Mission
Live the Life! Student Evangelism Training Kit
Make 'Em Laugh!
Purpose-Driven® Youth Ministry Training Kit
Real Kids Ultimate Discussion-Starting Videos:
      Castaways
      Growing Up Fast
      Hardship & Healing
      Quick Takes
      Survivors
      Word on the Street
Student Underground
Understanding Your Teenager Video Curriculum
Youth Ministry Outside the Lines

Especially for Junior High
Creative Junior High Programs from A to Z, Vol. 1 (A-M)
Creative Junior High Programs from A to Z, Vol. 2 (N-Z)
Junior High Game Nights
More Junior High Game Nights
Junior High-Middle School TalkSheets—Updated!
More Junior High-Middle School TalkSheets—Updated!
Junior High-Middle School TalkSheets from Psalms and Proverbs—Updated!
Wild Truth Journal for Junior Highers
Wild Truth Bible Lessons
Wild Truth Bible Lessons 2
Wild Truth Journal—Pictures of God
Wild Truth Bible Lessons—Pictures of God
Wild Truth Bible Lessons—Dares from Jesus
Wild Truth Journal—Dares from Jesus

Student Resources
Backstage Pass to the Bible: An All-Access Tour of the New Testament
Backstage Pass to the Bible: An All-Access Tour of the Old Testament
Grow for It! Journal through the Scriptures
So What Am I Gonna Do with My Life?
Spiritual Challenge Journal: The Next Level
Teen Devotional Bible
What (Almost) Nobody Will Tell You about Sex
What Would Jesus Do? Spiritual Challenge Journal

Clip Art
Youth Group Activities (print)
Clip Art Library Version 2.0 (CD-ROM)

Digital Resources
Clip Art Library Version 2.0 (CD-ROM)
Great Talk Outlines for Youth Ministry
Hot Illustrations CD-ROM
Ideas Library on CD-ROM 2.0
Screen Play
Youth Ministry Management Tools

Professional Resources
Administration, Publicity, & Fundraising (Ideas Library)
Dynamic Communicators Workshop
Great Talk Outlines for Youth Ministry
Help! I'm a Junior High Youth Worker!
Help! I'm a Small Church Youth Worker!
Help! I'm a Small-Group Leader!
Help! I'm a Sunday School Teacher!
Help! I'm an Urban Youth Worker!
Help! I'm a Volunteer Youth Worker!
Hot Illustrations for Youth Talks
More Hot Illustrations for Youth Talks
Still More Hot Illustrations for Youth Talks
Hot Illustrations for Youth Talks 4
How to Expand Your Youth Ministry
How to Speak to Youth...and Keep Them Awake at the Same Time
Junior High Ministry (Updated & Expanded)
Just Shoot Me
Make 'Em Laugh!
The Ministry of Nurture
Postmodern Youth Ministry
Purpose-Driven® Youth Ministry
Purpose-Driven® Youth Ministry Training Kit
So That's Why I Keep Doing This!
Teaching the Bible Creatively
Your First Two Years in Youth Ministry
A Youth Ministry Crash Course
Youth Ministry Management Tools
The Youth Worker's Handbook to Family Ministry

Academic Resources
Four Views of Youth Ministry & the Church
Starting Right
Youth Ministry That Transforms